LAURANCE WIEDE [illegible] 46. His other books in [illegible] Harm *Done* (poetry), [illegible] *William Wegman*, and *F* [illegible] *nelson*. He is co-editor [illegible] *English Inspired by the Bible*. He has published essays and reviews in numerous magazines, including *Partisan Review, Aperture, The New York Times Book Review, The Village Voice, Connoisseur, Camera Arts,* and *American Craft*. Founder and editor of Brightwaters Press and of Nimbus Books, he edited *American Craft* and *Camera Arts* magazines; he has taught at Cornell University, The Yale University School of Music, and Princeton University. He lives with his family in Patchogue, Long Island, New York.

CW01640495

Also by Laurance Wieder

The Coronet of Tours
No Harm Done
Man's Best Friend: Photographs by William Wegman
Full Circle: Panoramas by Kenneth Snelson
Chapters Into Verse: Poetry in English Inspired by the Bible

The LAST CENTURY

Laurance Wieder

SELECTED POEMS

Introduction by John A. Scott

PICADOR
AUSTRALIA

First published 1992 by Pan Macmillan Publishers Australia
a division of Pan Macmillan Australia Pty Limited
63-71 Balfour Street, Chippendale, Sydney

Copyright © Laurance Wieder 1992

All rights reserved. No part of this book may be reproduced or transmitted in any form or by any means, electronic or mechanical, including photocopying, recording or by any information storage and retrieval system, without prior permission in writing from the publisher.

National Library of Australia
cataloguing-in-publication data:
Wieder, Laurance, 1946- .
The last century.

ISBN 0 330 27322 1.

I. Title.

811.54

Typset in 10.5/13 pt Garamond by Midland Typesetters
Printed in Australia
by The Book Printer, Victoria

for
A&A

ACKNOWLEDGEMENTS

A number of these poems first appeared in Boulevard; Columbia College Today; Epoch; New Observations #43; New York Arts Journal; Nimbus Broadsides; Pataphysics; Poetry in Motion; Scripsi; The Little Magazine; The New Yorker; NO HARM DONE (Ardis, Ann Arbor, 1975); *Just Before Sailing;* THE CORONET OF TOURS (Ithaca House, 1972); *Buzzi Brueckner; Columbia Review; Paris Review;* and *Trojan Horse.*

CONTENTS

Wealth of Nations

The Exchange

INTRODUCTION

Three days after *The Last Century* was delivered to my *atelier* in Paris, I received a postcard from Laurance Wieder. He looked forward to meeting me that summer—an event which, due to my sudden impoverishment, never materialised. The card was postmarked PATCHOGUE NY MAR24'90 U.S.POSTAGE 0.45—the 0.45 preceded by three wavy lines, like a child's ocean. On the front of the card was the reproduction of a photograph attributed to A. Fernique, Paris, 1883. I'll describe it.

Within a large barn-like building, its space divided into several horizontal areas—raised platforms for working . . . endless mezzanines!—its floor littered with planks and timber scraps, are gathered some thirty-six men. Nearly all are wearing caps. Nearly all have beards. Throughout this working area are large tables covered with sheets of some material. Knowing nothing of the procedures being followed here, I have no idea what it is: leather, paper, metal?

The men stand amongst these tables. In their hands are mallets or hammers. In the right-hand corner, closest to the camera, a man holds what I imagine must be a mortar—though its appearance is as much that of a goblet of wine or a champagne saucer. Most likely he is seated at a table (his lower torso and legs are hidden behind the unknown material) though it is possible he is a dwarf. Apart from one man, whose face is blurred to a werewolf likeness, all thirty-six have remained scrupulously still for the camera. In this enclosure, over-determined with noise-making implements, there is an absolute silence. *But this is not the point*. Behind these men are the left hand, arm, shoulder and accompanying half-torso of the Statue of Liberty. Her hand holds a slab of stone. At the moment a vast *tabula rasa*. Towards the back of the room is an identical half-torso, only much reduced in size. Beside it, in identical scale, sit the head and shoulders of a *third* Statue. So much liberty.

Now this photograph is propped up on the desk of my study in Austinmer. And suddenly I realise that what Laurance Wieder had actually sent to me in Paris was a detailed metaphor of his own book—the kind of privileged reading that locates itself in introductions. I examine the photograph. I contemplate the pristine dialectic of its image: Europe and America; the Olympian and the human; the surreal and the quotidian; the *Declaration* and the common utterance; *The Word* and the word; the silence and the noise.

I turn back to his book: these are the new parables for the new cities, alert to other languages and other times. I consult Wieder's own "Curriculum Vitae": *Byron reborn as a suburban Jew . . . Blake with glasses . . . Rilke with a part-time job . . . Mallarmé in English . . . Horace, farmless*. The thing defined by everything it's not, Roman and romantic, visionary, symbolist: *Donne, but just begun . . . Marvell on asphalt;* the metaphysician's contemplative bent and accompanying wit directed to the streets, discerning in the raucous hooting of the seized-up intersection the music of the spheres.

And like some metaphysical conceit, the actors no longer walk us through their galleries to note Frà Pandolf or a Claus of Innsbruck bronze, but loom above us in the dentist chair: *"You know, there just might be a story in this, the story of a man a little different, reflecting on the everyday, life's foibles."* Here are the voices: the ordinary failures, the ordinary fears: *"I'm over forty, not so crazy anymore, and I think I will go back to teenage girls"; "Enough of me. How is your marriage? Things looked strained"; "Sir, may I ask you, how is it pronounced, serenity?";* interwoven with the truths of four-year-olds: *"There are two earths—the one that's dirt, and then the world";* the wisdom of the immigrant: *"We watch the television on the Watergate, but any country that give you only two choice for the election, what can you expect?";* or the *mauvaise foi* of Goofy: *"Only I could save them, but I stared like I was hypnotised and I didn't care".*

Hymn of praise or hypochondriac's lament. These are the tracking shots along Manhattan streets that might be taken from another *Annie Hall*:

> *Speech, too, is a wind of wickerwork*
> *Woven about the sense and feel*
> *Of things; the spirit's cage*

And the cause for wonder is this gracious interweaving; how the plenitude coheres; and how the English of *The Wanderer* could quite as easily be overheard upon the subway. There is a staggering versatility to this language: powerfully energetic verbs, a floor that *"thwarts"*, an economy that *"rises, waffles, bolts"*; a mysteriousness of nouns, allowing us to discover, like a child, *"honesty, Job's tears, sweet William, statice or sea lavender"* in a garden.

I look back to the photograph. Behind these ordinary people with all their histories and cultures stands the Statue of Liberty—perhaps as it must stand now (post-Vietnam, post-Chile), dismantled or diminished. And if there is a "truth" to Fernique's vision, it is that *Liberty* is a god made by men; a construct that can be disassembled at will—and all too easily—existing by these acts of faith, of industry, or of imagination.

I turn back to the book. All the gods are gone: Jahveh, Marx, the Dollar. Goofy brushes with despair, suffering his momentary *angoisse*, but managing to draw the line well short of *engagement:* in his dream of Mickey and Minnie chained to a rock and pushed over the cliff he is (unlike Propertius) quite incapable of even scaring himself awake! The void lurks: "a *New York City roof, or a rural gorge*". The big Disney mice have finally disappeared beneath the waves.

. . . I think of man's whole life
How it drops through the floor . . .
Where all days come to holes and falls. . .

says poetry's first exile. I can hear those words spoken in a thousand accents, immigrant or lover, worker or suburban Jew. What sustains us; what makes these poems rise above despair or cynicism is this act of faith, coupled with the power of imagination—the way the smoke entwined with Rabbi Simeon's pronouncement might come to be kept from falling, impossibly, by an eagle; imagination fuelled by innocence (the poet in his contemplation of the clouds; clear August day, the air smelling of apples); imagination delighting in resistances (for that is how we know ourselves):

. . . imagination.
That's why the floor
Supports us, why
It thwarts.

I look at this photograph. There is a gift being assembled here. It is a vision of the future. There is industry. And there is hope. I look at *The Last Century*. "The man is good who holds to his truth," says the oldest exile, in many voices. The longest walk through the streets of Manhattan brings us home. The doorman hands us a package from an undecided publisher. And messages are on the answering machine.

JOHN A. SCOTT
AUSTINMER, 1990

1

The Last Century

Pillow Book

Mild but wild, April day with winds
That make tall wavers of the cedars.
Peach buds wearing lipstick blow
Pink blooms. The Japanese dwarf plum,

'Abundance,' lags. 'Daddy, what is doom?'
Too many pillows give me a stiff neck.
To be famous in my lifetime
On another planet. On my own

I watched a seagull perch atop
A reed-bound piling, but damned
If I could sort the fruits by color
Or by number, or could match

The right word to its picture.
A tipped-in map, 'The Holy Land,' marks
The Twelve Tribes of Israel—(not
The edition with Christ's words

Spoken on earth shown in red ink.)
The picket fence repels all stranger dogs.
I could have answered, 'Girl,
Forget the hags,' as the nature

Of her question begs, but words died
On my lips, which threw kisses
In their pithy place, of monuments
Now pencilled in the landscape.

Punch and Judaism

Years pass like days, days
        Feel like years. At four,
My daughter beat the steamer pot
        With dowels, 'til the knoll
Grew Himalayan. Her Tibetan drum.
        October. Panicked crickets
Scattered where the rake tore up
        Dry thatch. The south face
Of that maple yellowed. Before,
        I turned my bicycle to watch
A purple mallow nodding in the cattails.
        Before that, I cut switches
From a willow just to whip the air.
        That was the time I wanted to be old;
Wanted to be tall, and to find wisdom.
        Last night the moon rose higher
Than the sun, the ground mum as pines
        Threw down their needles.
My daughter told me: 'Daddy,
        We will die together. Do not worry.
I am very old.' A muffler coughed.
        I struck a match,
And let her light the candles. One
        By one, the zeros dream:
One god; no true religion.

Ring, ring: 'This is the Center,
        The center of Shadow
And Life?' Wrong number. Ring:
        'We have you booked
For your departure. Check or charge?'
        The sycamore's

Bare branches craze the empty cup,
        A china glaze that spills
My upturned gaze back to the saucer
        Earth, which stretches
Truth, and southward to the water.
        'Daddy, sing. Your lullaby's
Too short. Please make it longer.
        Make it plain, an easy
Plan so I can understand.
        I want to fill
My cowboy boots with mistletoes;
        My soles will kiss the walk.'
We rolled big snow balls in a ring
        To make a fort.
We made a man. The wind kicked up.
        The sun grew weak, day
Gray with white tatters hung high
        In the air, white
On gray, like a gull in a gale.

'America's been ruined by
        The coffee break.
There's no need to be rich,
        Just to get by
In comfort. I thought I'd work
        Until I dropped,
But an old blockage in my heart
        Has acted up,
So goodbye, independence. The bills
        Are snow, the money
Water. Better get a job. You know,
        My father never said one word
To me 'til after I was twenty. He
        Was angry at my mother.
My first wife was a creature of her habits
        And those habits got

The best of her. I wanted to paint
        Pictures for stories, not
Build houses, but my brother ran the family
        Business down, so I did
What I knew. Daughters are not sons.
        When a date came to the house
To pick one up, I'd meet him at the door
        And ask, "Whose little boy
Are you?" Worked like a charm.'

The jays and cats are not amused.
        'At forty, you will have
No friends.' Not true. 'You've other
        Fish to fry.' 'Your own
Worst enemy.' 'You make a ghastly
        First impression.'
'Money's drawn to money.' Maybe.
        'You'll be dead
Before you're understood.' Not that.
        'You grasp at straws.'
'You're dreaming.' 'Fool.' 'A dish
        That I no longer eat.'

        'I ought to give up
Parties,' the survivor violinned,
        'Nothing happens
Once you're past the door.' That shuts
        Its ear, that breezes
Past my shoulder, beams at others, snorts,
        Withholds the love
The mother's child thought would never
        Sever, humble psalter
In a litany of numbers. 'Sledding covers
        Many motions, such as
Lying in the snow, and rolling over.'

'Have you got a minute? Do you mind
        If I (don't mean to pry)
Ask you a question about politics?
        Understand that in the 'sixties
I had long hair, too, smoked dope
        And walked through India.
When I was there I thought about a lot
        Of things, and since, I've started
Wondering, What if? What if, to take
        Just one example, revolutions
Going on right now in South America
        Were not just civil wars
But military actions funded by our enemies,
        The Russians, say, to weaken us
Just like the Right said they were doing all along?
        Suppose, to take it one step further,
That people for disarmament (and I
        Don't like nuclear war any more
Than you do), and those people are sincere,
        Suppose that nonetheless the Communists
Take full advantage of our system, which permits
        These idealists' dissent, and make
It serve their own agenda which is, say,
        World domination.
What would you say to that?'

My daughter named nine planets out
        Of order from today's
Dim sun, and shivered after every one.
        'There are two earths—
The one that's dirt, and then the world.'
        For her, the cartoon
Characters lived long ago,
        In history,
Like Pilgrims and the presidents.
        One starry night

She pointed to the bears, and asked
    'Where is the milky part?'
A man approaching seventy who gave up
    Smoking after fifty years,
Cut back martinis, upped donations
    To the temple, and devoted
His remaining days to tending assets,
    Doctoring his will, said:
'I felt better after all my teeth were pulled.'
    Or so the stars
Sang in my own cartoon, with death-
    Defying gravity
And solemn Solomon.

Because all the slow singers had died,
    We walked through
The dry snowfall. Evergreens
    Groaned in frozen
Daylight as the son and father
    Nodded, chatted
As if time had not yet passed
    Behind the hedges
Of their frosted picture. 'Don't
    Let on that I
Was here,' the older man repeated
    Through the taxi
Window. The car pulled into traffic
    And was not.
That's us, who know we do not know.
    The black cat, hunting
For a warm spot, played tom-toms
    On the door screen.
Serpents' new year, by the moon.
    My daughter said,
'The slow singers are all dead.
    The fast ones are

Alive. But one. Do you believe
        That song is true?'
I don't, but I like it, so I sing it.

King James Reggae

The mixed multitude kills time in Kingston airport.
Outbound flight delayed by bus wreck on the road.
        The last paper on the newsstand
        Sports a white girl's naked breasts.
A tropical depression's turned the Trade Wind to the east.

Our short hop across the island passed through
                                                            turbulence.
All week the downing of the innocents shook heads:
        The Gulf is an abyss:
                How many dead? Whose fault? Who swears?
A question thumbs its *Holy Bible* in the heat.

What is one man to do faced with such wickedness?
Such wickedness as lies
                                    cannot conceal? It had been
Twenty years beneath blue white red yellow stars
Since ball lightning pulsed while turtles climbed the
                                                                    beach.

The two-lane coastal highway reeked of cedar.
Hempfires whispered to the full moon,
        Fields of dancers chugged to train songs
                And old dreads, departed, swaying heads
Marked batswings in the air.
                                        Even now the Sunday radios
                                                                hosanna.

Human nature is one nation in the darkness.
There a bearded man stepped toward me in the shack
                                                                    light.
He peered into my face:

'Do you believe in the Most High?'
I could answer:
'Something larger and outside me.'

Shops do business. Children fidget on hot benches.
Older transients form a long queue at the bar.
Some change dollars; some write postcards; most
Just watch the airport monitors for word
When they'll be leaving where we are.

Mass Confusions and Enthusiasms

Like your psychology, my physics
Aspires to prose out the common magic,
To make something sensible
Of the invisible. Simple music
Must elude our logic, for the octave
Heard as moving upward through the scales
Registers only as a return, a circle
If graphed, on the oscilloscope.
In that gap between what's measurable
And felt live love and hope—the electricity
That flows about mortality
And charges fact, and makes it what we know.

Via Satellite

The moon waxed fat
From right to left,
A lawyer peeling
Off his suit
Of darkness. Commuters
Nodded on the rails.
I cracked the atlas
Open to a happy page
Where sand bars shrug
Tan shoulders, making
Surf. Judging only
By the map, the earth's
Grown older.
                    'The bill's
Right here.' The dog
Was forced to wait
Outside. A hazard,
Braking on wet leaves.
'Can you hold?'
                    'Can I
Get back to you?'
                    'I want
To be a bank next Halloween.'
Return to the Titanic, sinking
Rates, the evening meal, the sun
Setting below a shelf of purple
Clouds drenched with light
So potent that it cast no shadow
On tenements turned monuments.
One bears a sign: 'Third Rail'
        Painted lightning.
                'Can you bring

Two flashlights to the Tropics?
A percolator and appointment
Book? Wait. If I'm late,
It's a flat tire.'
                    October,
Each day fairer than
The next, and colder.
                              O suburb
Of the sun,
                O ocean, way
Beyond the bars that keep
The near bay calm, shine,
Gently scour the horizon
Of the autumn wader,
Of the winter clammer.

Downstairs on the Globe

Three weeks of cold
And Patchogue Bay froze
Over from the sandspit clear
To Fire Island. Mornings,
Gulls hop where once
They dove, and mew, and turn
Their noddy heads to follow
Baymen trudging 'cross the plate
Who stop, chop fishing holes,
Blow on their hands, drop lines,
And wait. The bay
Gleams black, pink, gun-metal, not
The fly's-eye mirror usual
But fixed, now, as the casual
Pickup driver parks on the pier
And aims his headlights south
Across the ice.

Goofy in the Middle

The phone rang late last night:
It was Mickey, wanting to sing me
Some song he'd just found about flowers.
I always try to stay up for the sports
Report and weather. It's hard
To make it through the news. Just think,
I could have run for President, or maybe
For Vice President, but Donald told me
That the best man wins, and Mickey
Never went for speechifying.
Babies sure are cute. Trouble is,
Since Mickey hypnotized me
Into thinking I was the Phantom Blot
And my unconscious mind led us
Straight to The Blot, my eyes close
By themselves, and I forget what happens next.
Mickey said, 'Let me sing this
Before I lose it.' It was a story
About Minnie and some morning glories
On her trellis Pluto used to sniff
Until some bees got mad and stung his nose.
One time I shook some salt on a bird's tail.
The bird flew off. An eagle. Maybe
If a Mexican guitar band strummed
The carioca and some señoritas danced
Before the first commercial, or I ate
Milk and cookies, I could stay awake.
But every time I go to dreamland
Earlier. Sure is lucky
Mickey called. I might have slept
All night in that big easy chair
With television on.

Goofy's Brush with Despair

I went out and bought myself
A new suit off the rack—
For a long time I'd been hoping
The right girl would come along—
But when I got back home
I looked in the mirror
And began to cry, and changed
Into my old clothes again.
I'm more comfortable looking
At where I've been than where I'm going.
As it says in this here book,
There's no way of telling whether
Other life exists beyond the stars.
It's mighty dark tonight.
I wouldn't sleep well knowing
Someone's staring down on me
From outer space. In fact,
I don't sleep well not knowing.
Last time I fell asleep I dreamed
That agents of a foreign power
Headed by Black Pete, had chained
Mickey and Minnie to a rock
And rolled it off a cliff
Into the ocean. Only I
Could save them, but I stared
Like I was hypnotized
And didn't care. I don't think
I could have saved them anyway.
At least I could have tried.
I'd better drink some lemonade.

Song

(from the Tamil)

A man may earn millions,
Dine with guests at fine restaurants,
Own cars, boats and houses,
Keep numerous mistresses,
Yet if he lacks children
Who toddle on carpets,
Who stretch out their tiny hands,
Throw food on the floor,
Smear the baseboards with paint,
Chew their fingers, their books,
And laugh as they step in
Their soft chocolate ice cream,
Then all of his days as a rich man
Are nothing.

Doubt Serene

The author of *The Incoherence of the Incoherence*
Must have recognized the stars' influence
On his prevailing fiction, though he probably
Didn't see diseases like influenza or anxiety
As symptoms of the lust for order, making
Metaphors of metaphor and mathematics into mastery

Of the soupy real by contemplative space. Mastery,
Then, like negatives of newsreels, makes of incoherence
An unrecorded counter-feeling which tries to influence
Those difficulties taken in the sun, probably
Succeeding only when the stars tick and anxiety
Rises, haze between the heavy trees and heaven,
unmaking

All that stellar certainty which was of one's own making.
Bare a white flank to the host of blankness, blanket
mastery
Over both the half-remembered childhood spent in
coherence
And scientific play, which has a half-uncovered influence
On what is done today—constellations of behavior
probably
Are our astrology. But no prediction comes without
anxiety,

Flux doesn't make me feel as snowmen do for flakes.
Against anxiety—
The thought one hasn't got it right—is making
Do with the materials at hand, repeating maybe mistakes
maybe mastery

Of those who take the body for a map of incoherence,
Framed by ice-glazed trees, that doesn't influence
The course it courses. Probably

All is as it should be, but I don't see it. Probably
Some defect in my faculties. Or is the method answering
anxiety
Different from the one that lets green hang in the air,
from mythmaking
And bookkeeping and getting and letting and betting?
Mastery
Then beams with native clearness, a lens through which
the incoherence
Shines like a silver fish of uncertain size, flashing in
fluence.

Down that transparence streams the bodied shadow of
the influence
Other pasts refer to the stars, or caring gods, improbably
Personal, but just as clearly addressed to the common
anxiety
To get it right for once. Here is darkness in the making.
Not to be afraid of it is all the mastery
I wish for, not to warp the darling incoherence.

For incoherence is the mother of all mastery,
Making whatever hope and happy influence
Bathes us. As anxiety's the freezing of disorder, probably.

Curriculum Vitae (1978)

Byron reborn as a suburban Jew,
Wordsworth after analysis,
Blake with glasses,
Keats recovered,
Shelley knowing how to swim,
Marvell on asphalt,
Donne but just begun, Ben
Jonson thin without Latin,
Hölderlin with a taste for Chinese,
Rilke with a part-time job,
Mallarmé in English,
Pindar of the aesthetes,
Horace farmless,
Dante stuck at home, and
        committed to short works.

Garden Intelligence

1

A stone bench in the cotton shadows.
First dew on the lawn, then dust. Someone is walking.
The heaviness the heaviness of clouds.
O cover us, and now and then disperse.
The bumble bee humming, 'Alas, how the thought
Drowned in overflowing,' and hovers.
The way a tulip falls apart, or a rose
Opens, or an anemone, to death—eternity
Looks like a rose, larger than a stadium,
With light where the bees would go.

2

And sing a song, a song I sing
Under the Tuba tree.
Whole Saturdays of sad pianos.
Of rowboats in the rain.
Blear mists, deep horns, light pocket sounds,
An echo of this or that.
And the dance, I dance
The elephant reel on rubber legs
To the cold coffee cup, to the melon, the stair,
To the cookie of contemplation.

3

Strawflowers, ornamental grass and other everlastings,
Honesty, Job's tears, sweet William, statice or sea
lavender.
Time's longer than the time of butterflies.
The monarch floats below the blue umbrella.

A monarch floats below the blue
Umbrella in the time of butterflies.
The redwing blackbird in the reeds
And other everlastings: a particle,
An ornament, like stars and what the thunder meant
With dark where the bees would go.

I Ate a Muffin and It was Enough

This morning waiting for my ears to clear
I thought about the lucent Milky Way,
Which rotates through the compass through the year

As though it were a cosmic ceiling fan
Churning atomic wind, that is, our time.
This morning, waiting for my ears to clear,
I thought about the lucent Milky Way.

At ten I knew the names of many stars
And thought the names were knowledge.
What to say? The names are far from me.
This morning waiting for my ears to clear
I thought about the lucent Milky Way,
Which rotates through the compass through the year.

Sitting in the dark can be a lark,
Like dancing to no music on a dare,
But in the end, the 'it,' it catches up

And one might wish one thing had been another,
That one had been less father and more mother.
Sitting in the dark can be a lark.
Like dancing to no music on a dare

The world goes round. At least, I hear no music,
See no spinning. Except their grand effects,
Which nowadays are the domain of science.
Sitting in the dark can be a lark,
Like dancing to no music on a dare.
But in the end, the 'it,' it catches up.

The greatest crimes are passions undetected
Which twist the great expanse into a knot
That only time may pass through unobstructed.

What does it matter that what passed for beauty
Was awkwardness decked out as a great seeming?
The greatest crimes are passions undetected
Which twist the great expanse into a knot.

The lever wants a fulcrum, life a heart
To see and saw the beam, its up and down:
The too thin sky, the none too solid ground.
The greatest crimes are passions undetected
Which twist the great expanse into a knot
That only time may pass through unobstructed.

The Last Century

The first fall day
In August, clear
The air smells like fallen apples
Around the reservoir
Where gulls sit mewing
On the same tempting blue that lured
The first Emperor of China out
To fish for the carp
Of eternal life.
He fell overboard, caught
Cold, and died.
We, too, are folded
In the chilly leaf,
Are drawn to the destructive moonrise.

Credulous, All Gold

An almost real speculation—parts
Will keep, parts
Drop. The lake in flood
O'erleaps, or rather, o'erlaps
Its banks, a full coffee cup
On a wobbly table.
                    Full of O's, mushrooms on October
Lawns, and how the leaves seem
Placed, as if on purpose.
                                        As if?
Cried the oriole. As if.

Harder to remove than a cranberry
Stain, it occurs
'That one thing, unsayable
But assumed—the self, perhaps
In its most reduced, elusive sense,
An initial, remains
Unwritable—allows one to think God's name
Unpronounceable, and god in man.'

Speech, too, is a kind of wickerwork
Woven about the sense and feel
Of things, the spirit's cage.
'Drop the bars, let it go, poor thing'—
But when that small bird escapes
As it will, who could tame it
Though it call out its name from afar?

Sparrows flock over a ballfield,
Staying on for the continent of winter
As the mother of all changes her clothes.

There is a time to huddle
Under hills indifferent to the wind
That tears them down, and a time to be drawn
Upward to an early bed.
Something is hanging in a tree: the thought
'Upon a leaf' and other gems
Of the external soul,
The rag a little person carries,
His talisman against the folds of darkness.

'Our sunrise in childhood is a candle in old age.'
'Your gorgeous language, guilt and restitution.'
The arras flaps. The wall is bare and cold.
'Decide. Are you a looker or a taker?'
'This napkin from Prince Henry's Portugal.'
I was there twice. They sold boats
Beaten out of gold and chased with silver
In the airport shop. The sun just risen,
The tarmac spackled by a sunrise squall.
But coming back the boy slept on through Lisbon,
And so farewell that westward with thy streams . . .

The child dreaded the day the sun would grow cold
And wondered what life was for, then,
And what people would do. Before
Came that beginning, that happened long ago.
And draws back, the way a wave curls back
To show the bottom, or the bottom of the wave.

Beyond the city limits, beyond
In fact the city of the mind with its own
Crowd- and cloud-capped towers, surges, electricity,
Stands a vacant plain, where one
Is just the size one is, and distance
Brings forth things without comparison.
No shadows there, unless one hold a light up.

No darkness there, unless one's eyes are closed.
All still. Such starry music. Windy tremors.
A pebble's been displaced.
The worm labors in darkness.

Measure, measure, measure, measure,
Measure out the days.
Card the cat and marry the canary.
Mop the floor.
Turn out the lights.
Fold the lofty linen up.
Our lives are rock.
The clear days water.
The air a thought.
A breath the border.
Measure, measure
Years brought by on trays.

Very soon I shall enter bitterness.
Very soon the sights will turn to windiness.
And soon the street,
the low grade's gentleness
Descends the omnibus
That cometh after us.

Raft on a row of air.
We stay. The sun goes by.
Stars later. You and I
Are better when such things
Inside us glare. Pillows.
Sheets that slake.
The earth a bed.
The air a lake
For a time calm smooth.
By the time we notice
They stay, we move.

At night the covers close
Sweet face, so you need look no more.
No more upon the cashmere days,
On clouds that ride the veil shoulders,
On Demeter crushing beetles, sowing grain,
On windows stained with ivy,
Windfall, landfall, footfalls in the hallway
And no one before or behind.
A horse stomps in the emerald blast.
The shadows fall in colors,
Themselves degrees of darkness,
As Helios rings for his whetstone,
As a man taps his gold-tipped umbrella.

I know how I want it to end.
As it began, in silence
And the drift of a large impatience.
As though, arms down, refusing
To fly one could transcend
Not the arrangement
But the distance between bare trees
Beckoning the pomegranate sun
To mount yet lower in its solemn space
And that transmitted firmament
That when I speak up turns
To cream swirls, smoke in a teacup.

The dead fold their umbrellas
And call for the gods, who remain
Beyond the hollow sprinkling crumbs
Of light on shades afflicted
With a rapture of the shallows.
Shallow as a building in a puddle,
Shallow as Sarmatians sweeping over,
Shallow as the arch of an eyebrow,
Shallow as the full moon in a bare sky,

In a watercolor of Korean moonlight.
There, too, snow falls into the colorist's water,
A tern paused in imagined flight.

Finish Up

A leaf, when torn, becomes
An instrument the wind plays
Airs on, no repeats
But in bits, where no one
Movement says it all, and
What's vocalized vanishes,
Leaving what fits.

Animal, vegetable, mineral:
A botany student recorded his dream:
    I sat at a table, wondering
    What is it?
    Where is my ego?
    —a feeling most uncomfortable.
Animal, vegetable, mineral.

Swiss Independence Day

At sunset, the campers take
Their shingle boats down to the lake
And, lighting candles, let them drift
Out toward the middle. Weak as stars left
In the city, their liquid pin lights
Snake and gutter, wax and white.
Little did the homesick boy
Suspect a time would come when
He would feel homesick for then,
Or that the tapered fleet that Alpine night
Would feel more permanent than clay
Dogs modelled by his daughter,
Than teenage love and what came after,
Than the bathtub at his feet.

How nice to soak and rhyme a quarter hour
Away in a hot shower:
The morning sun makes rainbows in the spray.
To win the lottery you have to play.
Between the steamy billows and the solid
Porcelain's our world, *The Book of Pillows*,
Where 'Man is Free' as ornamental
Pear trees shaken slightly by the wind.
They demonstrate the trunk and root
Are real, and though the foot
May catch, the dancer fall, the lake
Swamp the candles, it's no mistake.

A Song that Lies The Least to the Most

A gray lady on the subway
        Touched my sleeve:
'Sir, may I ask you, how
        Is it pronounced,
Serenity? And the noun,
        Serene?' I answered
As the dictionary
        Would, and added,
'Easier to pronounce
        Than to attain.'
She thanked me, saying
        'Do you know
The prayer: "Lord, give me
        Strength to bear
What I can change, serenity
        To accept what I
Cannot . . ."'
                'Yes.'
        'Do you know
How it ends?'
                'No.'
        '"And the wisdom
To know the difference."'
        She took a piece
Of broken mirror from
        Her purse, and fixed
Her face.
                When I was young
        And had to chase
The girls, I caught them, crying
        'I'm a poet'
To sound interesting.

Decades passed. Now tuned
For others' voices to record
I find I'm duller
Than I ever dreamed. What's more,
It doesn't hurt.
'This won't hurt. Hold still.
Which is worse:
To kill a fly's head on
The body of a man,
Or to swat a man's head
On a fly's body?'
I thought of sex the way
I think of money:
If only I could get
Enough. Enough,
And only that. An American
History professor
Discovered after forty
Years that women
Were not meant for him,
Nor he for them.
Before getting on
The red-eye to
New York to tell his mother
What she never
Guessed at, should have known,
He phoned: 'I'll start out
"Mother, I have good news . . ."'
'Don't say "good news"—
She'll think you have found Christ.
Stick to the facts.'
'Good point. I'll tell her, "Mom,
I've learned something
About myself that gives me
Hope, for life."
My sister's so annoying.

When she calls she
Always tells an AIDS joke.'
Depressions, wind,
The yellow bone of time:
An understated
Melody hounds the sculptor
To his basement
Shop to tinker 'til
He finds, or hopes
To find, those blissful pools
He splashed in
Before three, when 'that woman
Had not yet made
Her true self known to me.
The lack you noted
Is my mother. Catch
You later.'
Even now
I think about my father,
Demented in Eden,
Getting children he
Will never nurture:
Ferocious, the reverse
Of praying mantis,
Backed into a corner.
'Your face is bathed
In golden radiance,'
The portrait taker
Said, capping his lens,
And smiled, thinking
How his shot would look
Between hard covers.
I will not dispute
Another's vision.
Seated on his desk,
An algebra

Teacher demonstrated
        Practically
The meaning of the term
        Parabola
By tossing sticks of chalk
        One by one
Onto the floor, saying
        'Parabola'
Each time. They came in white
        And took him off.

'Save the Phenomena'

That two-ton tomcat, yet again
Scampering across the keys,
Tilted the embroidered birds locked
In their golden frames. It's
Raining, pouring, dumptrucks
Shake the turntable, so the microtonal
Music sounds like leaky lapstrake
Through a microphone. What message?
Rapped out on the board, direct
From where to here? O blossoms
Beaten by the clouds' tattoo
That dot the dragon-chested asphalt
With a map of some near galaxy
Craving to be heard below
Transmission waves, for years
That travel faster than earth days
Blown through the yellow clarinet
In March, out the conservatory window:

I set aside my paper calculations,
Which only cluttered anyway
The voyage out of space, though not yet
Out of time. The two-year oracle
Has spoken: 'No more poets,
Laughing Boy.' This while plucking
Live leaves from the potted fig tree
After lunch, and what she meant
Won't translate out of cold spring gray
Into the speech of hemlocks, hollyhocks, hydrangeas
I predict will burgeon
Along building sides, but I'm sure
It was no joke.

Flagstone

1

Walking past an iris
Yesterday I thought:
My eye is in love
With this iris, but
How can we live this way?

2

        Folding the Hudson's Bay
Blanket that cushions
        The seat of the prickly rattan,
My daughter said: 'A half,' and
'Daddy, if we eat, we will not die.'

3

Better even than the scent of camellias,
Than the dense cloud of night-blooming jasmine,
Than the tea air of roses, the rock of wisteria,
Is the smell of fresh cash. Himalayan spring.
Able to have everything; able to need nothing.

4

        Though I knew from the start
There was no living in it,
        I chose poetry.

Though I knew
There is no love without
Parting, I chose you.

5

That night a highway
Crew came in a cherry-picker
Crane and changed the dead
Bulb in the streetlamp to one
The color of moonlight.

6

At the National Academy,
The Buddhists all wore business suits
And mixed their orange juice with sparkling water.
At the Botanic Garden, bees
Try overpowering a flaming peace rose.

7

And I do remember yesterday,
How you waited patiently
To music that they danced to in the old days:
Three crows sitting on a maple limb
Drive the starving strays away.

Your Melodies

God is so angry with us
That he takes our wits before
He takes our life. This candle,
Guttering, should last about as long
As my supply of music paper, always low,
And my pen runs slower than the melodies
Spill out. My father reckoned I could teach
The alphabet and figures for a living, anything
Else I wanted to depend upon my salary.
That's how the world goes. On the other hand
I hear the praise of a deaf master, and every
Second thought loops in that measure
Bridegrooms dip to, into laughter
Dapping like a troutline on the working waters.
And then I'm out of time,
Don't even know if I am wearing glasses.
The songs make what's inside of things
Come out, the table legs wear dancing shoes,
And millstones grind in matrimony slowly,
But exceeding fine. I have to have
My little puns. They trouble
Neither God nor the convictions of the choir.
I need to walk along the avenue
And drink in like a mannikin the fables
Played before shop windows, listen to the gypsies
Hawk their versions of a future gleaming
In the ball of chesty hope and murky fate.
I must go out, I say, but some pain
Pins me to this chair, and keeps me
From out there, as though the scene
Were but superfluous attachments

For a rare machine. But when I go,
Perhaps to eat a meal, down
A glass of beer, and meet and greet
Those friends I still see frequently,
And even those who crop up after many years
At a funeral or wedding, after shaking
Hands and wishing well, I taste
The ashes of a former flame, the tremor of old slights.
And I'm at my wits' end.
And don't know what it means.

Is That All?

'Six month ago I was a rich man
And I don't know it: I have
Freedom, money, house, the family . . .
Today, that's all gone crack. Today
Is Easter and the Passover.
Do you believe in God? I say
It all depend on what you mean.
If you mean God is someone I
Must love so he look out for me
Then I say "No, I don't believe."
From when I was a little boy
Of nine year old at dinner with
The mother and the father—in Trieste
Where people kneel to the Pope—
I know there is no God.
                    Church
Is okay to meet the girl
To marry, like a club, but I think
Jesus was no real man, you understand,
Because at that time Jewish people
Marry young, boys at fifteen,
But Jesus never marry. Who he hire
To work with him? The fisherman.
In Trieste everybody know
Nobody stupider than fisherman.
Today nine year ago I go
Into the hospital for operation.
That time I think, "I'm dead.
Seventy-six." But no, today
Is I stand here, and Henrietta
Is the one.

When I come to
This country, in five month I speak
The English better than I do now
After sixty year. What the hell.
Is not important no one understand me.
You know, I could do anything,
Go visit Europe if it was
Just me alone. Like yesterday
Was beautiful, I want to fish—
All time I love the fishing—
But no more. Instead I sit
Beside the bed, three in the morning
If she call.
Look, Peter come.
Peter, you are the half and half,
Half Christian and half Jew.
Is lucky, you can take your pick.
To me the holiday is just like Christmas
To the child who don't believe
In Santa Claus: he don't expect
But maybe he still want the present.'

Happiness is my Beat

My head aches, my right arm twinges, my stomach gripes
and roils—
I will close my eyes just for a moment
I will take off my glasses and nap for an hour
I will curl up and sleep until morning
I will stay in bed for a day, for the week, for a month,
until spring, until autumn
I will not get up again
I will close my eyes and lie down forever

Infatuation

Just thinking about being
Dead at my age gives me
A headache: there was poker

With Ted gulping dope and drink
Roaring: 'Two aces, fuck a pig's butt'
(I don't think he was bluffing)

And, by report, by my age
All his teeth fell out, he only got
Up from bed (off the couch)

For a dump, or an interview, a shot
Of whatever. Then he was not.
On the other hand, I wrote a letter

To a dying friend this June as though
He were already dead. I took
Advantage of his foreknown doom

To say things left unsaid in the five years
Since last we spoke. Told him
I loved him, cursed the joke

His body'd played on him, on us, and closed
With him ever in my thoughts at Passover
And other turns God takes. Why bother

When there are no grapes to gather?
Why gape at clusters dewed from the refrigerator?
The swag lamp ticks. The ceiling fan on low.

A big hand for the little fellow, grappling
The ghost of his not-dead father.
I dreamed about him Friday night,

Walking barefoot through the cotton shade
In shorts, a toddler dawdling behind . . .
The child peered into a coconut husk

Tossed against the wall of conch shells
A few steps from the beach. No way to reach
Whatever web he'd spun inside the hut,
To know if he was lying in the bed he'd made.

I woke up without the headache
Of an unremembered dream, and vowed
Aloud I'd write a letter. Forty now,

I may know better. But the barometer
Has sunk below complaint, while the heat—
Archtypical July—has stopped

The fluted edges of what's owed.

Some Horses and Some Cows

A bow tie, a green bow tie with sparkles:
Tuck it under my chin like a violin.
Stop crayoning that singing salamander.

The cloud in my mouth tastes like yogurt.
Let me look at the moose on your beer.
I have no cup. I can't say 'Cheers.'

Help! there's an ant on my socks, and
Roar! the lion has made a design, but
Don't be afraid, it's a friendly lion.

What a relief. Is that the whole moon
In the sky? Bye-bye, I'm going to Bombay
To see some horses and some cows, and sleep all day.

Blow out the candle in the pumpkin, bumpkin.
No kissing on my cheek, just kissing
On my back. I said, no kissing

On my back, just kissing on my knees.
Not both knees, only kissing
One by one. No talking. And no looking.

Fame

Dinosaurs died with meat on their bones
Dinosaurs died with meat on their bones
With their feet in the mud
                    they turned into stones
Except for the ones that grew feathers

The Mystery of the Moroseness of Geoffrey Hill

(1989)
by Urizen Lamb

Gadzooks! abandon Krazy Kat? snub Daffy
Duck? Th-that's all, folks. Hand organs grind
Out hymns of praise. The cranks don't understand
Nothing's funny. Black and white, the coffee

Shudders, overflown blue cup of Delft
Ware, bombed out by a rising middle class
Of scented, dusted, medicated grace-
less grocers shaving ounces, loving wealth,

Meat, chintz—suntanned carrion unlike
Thy faithful servant Geoffrey Hill: morose
Yet boring. Inhuman family of cheese
Sayers at a picture-taking, chalk

Squeaks on slate, half-lit professors cheer
Lugubrium. Pamplona's bullring thunders
'¡Viva la muerta!' Taurine, truth's untender
To the lone reader, who gulps no glass of beer

At mirth's saloon, crabbed but his own
Dreams' mouthpiece, tooting poetry through horn
Of horny harvest mysteries still born
Upon this strait earth corporations own.

Did Hill kill joy? Harrowing, his hell
Hounds gnaw at unresurrected bones
Of prophets bundled off in paper chains:
Forged rules, minds forged, fools manacle

Themselves to victor-doctored histories
Bent only on hosannas to the present

Rot, a fat cat's furred purr of content.
Just one just man can mortify these stories

Back to painful life. 'Be solemn, now
A fool approaches.' Crowds, an audience
Desires an old man's incontinence,
A scourge. The headsman lays it on, and how!

And howl, weep, Jerusalem, a footnote
Telegraphed bouquets time dashes at
Clay feet. The smoking banker tushes at
Frederic Chopin's *Polonaise* of hope

With grunt and wheeze, defiant public sex
Last practised in the Nineteenth Century
By girls named George and their transparent boys,
Who may have been consumed by its effects.

Return, decorum. Gird, thou rigid forms
The corset-wanting waist of sloppy joys.
Let men be men, girls girls and stern be poise.
Abolish by compression the lapsed norms,

The porno pansy, hard faith's nemesis . . .
'Come off it, Geoff,' the blissful tempter hissed,
'By sixty, sins become what you have missed
While penning your parthenogenesis.

You've fled, like Dracula, first light, last
Native land, to smelt in somber Boston
Dark ore among the remnants Puritan,
Condescendent. The end can't come too fast.'

The bard rejoined, 'Over-familiar offal
Of the mart, go south on Madison
Avenue: an agency can bare your bosom
There. Great gloomies relish mine.' Life's awful

Heavy hanging over Beacon Hill.
Rare the eye won't blink at truth, terrific
Doom. O moth, stay out of highway traffic.
Those drivers titter, stuffed in shirts that kill.

The Map of Japan

'We're just a couple nearly forty
With a baby and no money
In the bank. This isn't Larchmont.'
And this isn't parchment.

This isn't parchment, yet it's paper
Largely floats our modest venture.
Debt's a caper to our credit, both
In earnest and a figure with no matter.

So, guilt hedges the security. No matter what,
The last fall trees turn colors from the top
Down, in three strata—archæology
Of the unexcavated future, yours and mine.

It isn't yours, it isn't mine, save
For the moment. Chinese characters
Blocked by the sun on red brick walls stir
Up a calligraphic, watercolored feeling

In another tongue than this, which puns
On the great whoosh, the crack, the sweeping
Backwash of a creeping race. Asleep,
Or half-asleep, I watched the bamboo

Shadows of imperfect glass, the shutters
And the trees outside play on the nursery wall
Cast by the passing headlights, and I thought
No thought except the sight, as painters

Might if painters with an oriental bent
Had kept my bottle vigil
In the watches of the night, and all
Their difficulties were just mental.

If all my difficulties were just mental,
Would they be on the wall map of Japan?
The watchword among nations Hiroshima,
The cresting wave, the bullet train,

Love suicides, a broken spray of pear, all
Spare and untranslated? Teenagers are elated
By art and music, which will never die, at least
No more than we do, shaking dice and humming

'Merrily we roll . . .' 'Row, row . . .' by rote, on faith.
Before the last malignant habit's turned
To smoke. Hooray. Just knuckle
Down to work today. Eat something. Practise

Pirouettes, tune up your instrument
And make it good, or new, or what you will.
If not, then worship as the city
Pigeons do, in wheeling flocks

Above the towered altars of the clouds.
No heaviness allowed, no tense or gory
Spectacles—just retell a modest story
Brushed by the coatsleeves of the crowd.

2
Wealth of Nations

Chorus

Do not begin far from us
Death is yet near to us
Darkness, and crying, and rust and dismay

In the small rose, the heart
Calls the bee to its part
And the bee sucks its pollen, and flies away

Julia Bloomfield

24 June 1974

Days are skirts, and years the wind that raises them.
Who sees the white ankles time shows, praises them.
Time is the great parter
Of the waves, of people straining for the garter.

That's an airy conceit,
But Julia is steady on her feet,
Tending the garden
Days, so they don't harden.

Watching flowers, she becomes them,
Slightly tongue-tied (in dreams all's not said)
And even if she sums them
Up, they're only flowers in a flower bed.

Time is the great collector. It's brought
Us together for a birthday, no more serious
Than anything else that's been remarked, or thought.
As life gets older, life gets more mysterious.

Anatomy

' "You talk in rhyme, it always sounds
Like rhyme," she said, and I replied
"It sounds like rhyme because it's right." '
'You can use that,' Chuck observed.
'There was this problem, then, between us—
The intelligence . . .' He stroked his goatee
Once then trilled his fingers in the air.
'And she had little secrets. Like her name.
We lived together for three months before
She told me that her name was not the one
She went by at the go-go bar.
I told you how we met? A friend
And I went to this topless bar in Queens
Where, between the pinball
And beer mugs banging in the bar sink,
By strobe light, I saw her
Flash G-string and pasties, Queen
Of Sodom, as it were, wreathed in her power.
I exaggerate. Anyway, she stepped down
For her break. We got to talking.
I had never known someone like her
(Her mind I mean), so when my friend
Said he was leaving for the City,
I took a chance, and stayed.
She got off work at 4 a.m. She had a car.
When I suggested she could drive me home,
She looked me in the eye and said,
"You could be a pervert." I said,
"You could, too, and I'm not worried
About me." Anyway,
We drove back to Manhattan and sat talking
Parked near the entrance to my building

Until one in the afternoon.
Next time, she came upstairs.
We lived together for three years.'

He sipped his brandy. 'The thing between us
Got more difficult, showed up
In funny ways. Like giving presents.
Once, a month before my birthday,
We went to the Francis Bacon show
At the Metropolitan. It made her nervous—
Didn't stay long—but I said
Before we left that if she ever
Wanted to give me a gift, I'd like
The catalogue. The morning of my birthday
She went out for several hours, came back
With a package, put it in the closet,
Left for work. I knew what was going on,
Said nothing for two weeks, then took
The book down from the shelf. She said,
"Oh yeah, happy birthday." I said, "Thanks."
We fought a lot. She didn't wash. We fell apart.

'Some months after we split up
A lady friend of hers and mine said
They had come by my apartment
When I wasn't in, and Wren
Had gone inside and stayed there
For an hour. But everything was
In its place, so I filed the incident,
Figuring its meaning would become apparent.

'One year later I was cleaning up
Before I moved my stuff up to the country
When, behind the radiator in the living room,
I found a note—that
Accounted for the hour.

It said (I will not quote):
"I was here, but you were not.
I wanted to tell you you were good
For me, to touch you once more just
To say goodbye." I put that note
Into a painting, to show her
She was part of me, but the one time
We met, by chance, she spat in my face.

'That was, I guess, my last romantic love.
I'm over forty, not so crazy anymore,
And think I will go back to teenage girls.'
'Some story, no?' Chuck said,
And we three talked at length
About the power naked women have.

California

One afternoon in the lounge of the Gem Institute
A young woman in short skirt and high boots
Sat near me with a cup of coffee.
I said to her: Don't get upset.
It's nothing that I can't control,
But I confess I have
                    a mild foot fetish.
And she replied: Shall I put my feet in your lap?
    Oh, yes.
            And she did.
Later I overheard her talking to her girlfriends.
It was the most exciting thing to happen to her
Since she came to California.

                    Read to me,
Young lady, read to me this passage from *Justine*.
I've closed the office door,
The principal's away at a convention,
And I trust there's little stronger than the bond
Between a junior high school teacher and his student.

Foxglove, Source of Digitalis

'I know an old woman
Who sleeps with a hammer.
She worked all her life
As a waitress, and saved
Until now she has jewels,
Owns a condo in Florida,
Put her one boy through medical school.
The son has a good practice
In obstetrics, in New York, but he
Betrayed her: he married
A woman. The old mother
Keeps their wedding portrait
In her pocketbook, and shows it
Every chance she gets, saying:
"See that woman smiling?
Why shouldn't she smile?
She married a doctor."
And raps the chair arm with her bangle bracelets.
Which brings us to the hammer.
The waitress had a premonition
She would die in the night
Of a heart condition.
At bedtime she lays out her diamonds
And pearls on the night-table.
With her last gasp she plans
To smash all her jewellery
So she can die knowing
Her son's wife won't wear it.

'I love to quote poetry
As I make the grand round
And after, at the daily

Mortality session. You know,
Not an intern could tell me
The name of the poet
I quote—(he wrote
"Do not go gentle into that . . .")'

The Wild Banana, Our National Flower

'I raised two children:
One girl when I was seventeen;
One boy when I was thirty.
Their father ask me: "Gerry,
How come you never marry?"
Marry? I say, "You get me
With two babies
But your wife get six."
What for? And I am through
With him now twenty-seven years.

'Two years ago last April
My daughter writes a letter:
"My father is dying."
You know, I stand
Upon my hands and do
No thing. The car's not made
Could drive me to that funeral.
This is my lifetime speaking:
You must enjoy yourself
And wait to marry.
Now I want to live
Just to myself alone
In the hills, some few
People bring me work.
And that is all.'

The old washerwoman sat
Telling me what she thought
Was the heart of the mystery.
She waved her hands about
Her head and fixed one swollen eye

On the cigarettes, the ashtray, blown
With shadows of the squallish clouds,
And laughed as I leaned forward.
Chin in hand, I nodded
And puffed, never hearing a thing
For the roar of the mower
Below the verandah, figuring
She was talking mostly
To the gone away,
Or to the sunlight strong
Enough to shrink a coconut,
Or to the plantain shadows,
Where the doctor bird
Touched flower after flower.

Art History

I said to the psychiatrist:
I feel depressed.
He said:
You've left your wife,
You're living in a dump,
Your dog is dying.
If you didn't feel depressed
You would be crazy.
I remember one large fight we had,
Pearl smashing glass and tearing
All my work down from the walls.
She shook a sketch pad underneath
My nose and screamed:
Paper, paper, paper, paper,
Everything you do you turn to paper.
And she had a point.

The Paradise Rug

When we woke up at 7:30, it snowed
Last night. I thought the bedroom
Preternaturally warm at 3:00 a.m.
And it was: snow's the proof. You left
For work at the music factory, saying
'Meet me at the church at 12:10 for Purcell,'
And locked the door. I dreamed of snowy parks
And haircuts through mid-morning, as the snow turned
From paper plates to urban glop. Last night
I read you *L'Allegro* and *Il Penseroso*
And you fell asleep, but I didn't mind
Because I left the storied towers of Manhatto
For a time, and entered the pure feeling
World, where feeling is thought, and shade
The color of windows from the street at sunset
Grows, quiet, happy. I could bless the known
Stars and houseplants freshly sprayed, then,
My days stretched like an archipelago, and large
And small, or neatly pressed between the leaves.
But back. You wore a green coat in the pew
As I blew in at the homily, a cloud.
They knelt. We kissed. Two Purcell anthems,
A prayer for management and labor in hard times,
Then to a counter for a cup of coffee. You were sorry
To bring me out into the weather, but I didn't mind
Because it took me once again
Into the *mysterium tremendum*, and to you.
                    In the center of my room
Is a paradise rug, and everything but poetry
Is like sex between small children, of no use
To them or us, save as a pastime. Four o'clock.
The key in the lock. The chains untwisting.

Dear Abby

Dear Abby:
                    I have met a boy,
A sculptor with a fine blonde crew cut,
Orphaned, versed in mathematics, winner
Of a statewide science fair at seventeen
Who understands my inner nature.
Once, I kept strict orthodox
And rose each midnight to address
My prayers to God in his chosen tongue,
Shunned pork, and stayed clear of my wife
When she was bleeding. That was easy. Lord,
Who am I? Who are other people to me?
Can we be fathers and be fair?
These doubts tormented me.
They drove me out of business
Into art, which is no place for little boys.
Can he be faithful? Or do men who love men always
Kiss and tell? My wife will take me back,
But I don't want to wrestle with my nature
For a lifetime. Is it true we die
And nothing gets left over, neither spouts
Of ecstasy nor bitter flakes?
If so, then what's the point?
I have bought the boy his own apartment,
One with northern light. Should I
Pay the utilities, or should he
Take some responsibility
Which would teach him to grow up,
The value of a dollar,

And just how much I really mean
To him?
    —Rapt in Manhattan

Rapt:
    It's better if you make him pay
The monthly maintenance.
You take the mortgage, which can be
A tax deduction. Ask your wife
What else she needs to keep her comfortable
For rest assured, there is no better peace
Than a household in good order.
You are your own best judge.

Poet, Pick Up that Guitar

A friend whose name translates as 'honorable'
Told me about a couple he stayed with
Outside Boston:
                    Dan the husband, played
Around with other women and his wife,
Barbara, stood for it, to keep intact
The family unit for son Josh.
Dan had his own true love in New York City
Named Barbara (ruling out
A possible confusion), and always came home
For breakfast, every morning.

Aside: Dan was compulsive. He collected
Every book he came across
Written by a 'Dan.' He said:
'I have a thing about my name.'
His father's name was Dan.

One evening Barbara, Dan and Josh ate dinner
At Dan's parents' and stayed over.
After the families retired, Dan
And his mother stayed up drinking vodka
In the living room. His mother, out
Of nowhere, started telling Dan how she
Felt horny and could not decide
Whether to use her hand or go down
To the corner bar and hustle up
A one-night stand. Dan blanched.
His mother said: 'Enough of me.
How is your marriage? Things look strained.'
Dan droned about his Barbaras and breakfasts.
His mother struck her head and groaned:

—'I should have told you. All my friends
Who knew said I should tell you.'
—'What?'
—'Years ago I had a brief affair
With another man. That man's your father,
Dan, not Dan, and now the pattern reappears
And you will wreck your marriage.'
—'You don't know. I never told you. Mother,
Josh, I'm not his father.'

Navigating through the fog,
The melodrama, many captains
Use an aid: triangulation.
It would appear less neat, less dangerous
To cast this tale in prose, as fiction,
But nothing fits together half so well
In fantasy as in imagination.
That's why the floor
Supports us, why
It thwarts.

Emblem

A shadow box where Pierrot
Strums a guitar and serenades
His femme, his fool, his fantasy—
The moon is full, it pulls the strings,
Unwinds the works of *Claire de lune*,
Of dangled engines of a dance
Done in despite, in means and moans—
Small chips of light, of heart, of sound.
All sparkles in the air, and clatters down.

Wealth of Nations

'Economics, Andrea, my love
Is like psychoanalysis: a science
Of the darkly understood. Look—'
(Pointing to the frog-voiced vagrant
Seated on the sidewalk who sells
Ball-point pens to passersby on Second
Avenue)—'a depressed man doing
Depressed business in a depressed time.
With insight into self or spending money
He might be there—' (pointing
To that radiant wedge, the Citicorp tower,
Just then chiselling a low cloud)—
'Or maybe not.'
                                        We wandered on.
'Consider. Money is completely human.
No god invented ready credit; no god
Or priest can gloss the whole economy.
It goes its own way, rises, waffles, bolts
Down Wall Street, a tide with its own rules
Like the unconscious. You have heard the story
Of the three philosophers engaged
In a dark room to explicate the elephant,
An animal they'd never seen? One grasped
The trunk, and said, "An elephant's a hose
Venting moist air." The second, underneath
Its stomach, said, "The beast's a hairy leather
Canopy." The third demurred: "We have
Here pillars crudely formed, and creaky."
Prolific metaphoric bulls and bears,
Street humors, panic, overconfidence
And current numbers for the navigator
Dot maps of that uncharted sea,

Stretched at the edges, the economy.
But on these figments real ills attend:
Hunger, idleness, despair.
Yet like the deep neurotic bound to his
Compulsive round, the patient can be helped
Through insight, healthy vigor of the mind.'
'Oh, come on,' Andrea said, as we stepped over
A derelict's crossed legs while he slept
On a cardboard mat over the exhaust
Grate of a Park Avenue bank,
'This talk will never keep us from the poorhouse,
As my mother used to say. Or,' skirting
An unscooped poodle poop, 'from starving
Like dogs in the gutter.'
                                        I laughed.
'Fears. Family fears.' Crosstown traffic essayed
Gridlock. 'America's no place for nervous
Nellyism. Look in this shoestore window.
For ninety dollars you can buy
A pair of sneakers that perform the same
Work as a pair available for seven ninety-five
At any upper Broadway discount shop.
But the ninety-dollar pair is more efficient,
An investment in our children's future
Way of life.'
                    'I thought we had to save
To send them to good schools,' my loving chuck
Replied.
                'The thought's naive, if not subversive.
                    Industrial societies
                    Thrive on efficiency.
                    Efficient production,
                    Efficient consumption:
                    Each begets the other.
That's the beauty of the high-priced sneaker:
One thing for the price of ten.

Why pay less when you can pay more?'
We passed a drugstore dressing up
Its windows for the Christmas rush.
'As Jesus said, you lose your soul
To find it. And the meek inherit. Paradox,
But central to our being
Here. That's Marx's failure:
He saw contradictions bringing down
The superstructure around our bourgeois ears.
In fact, they are the wit, the dash, the *verité*,
The glue. Glum Karl Marx
No better comprehends this Christmas shopping
Than—' (We passed a bank that offered
Cut-glass bottles filled with gumballs
To new depositors, plus high-cost loans)
'Than disco banking.'
                                        The sidewalk on Fifth
Avenue was blocked. Two three-card monte
Dealers and an arab hawking 'Bullwhips,
Six dollars, genuine leather,' drew a crowd
Of get-rich-quick suckers and seekers
After the odd bargain. 'Poor sheep, chasing
Chimeras when they could be spending, making
More to earn. If only . . .'
                                        'Nyah,' snarled
A short man wearing chains, 'why not go back
Where you came from.' And the crowd turned ugly.
'That will do,' my love said, hauling me away.
'It's bad enough you haven't got a job;
I don't need you dismembered.'
                                        'Hold on. I work,'
I said, stung. 'No one pays me, true,
But with no money come no money problems.
My mind is clear, my spirit's up.
Remember when I went in to an office

Every day: no windows, headaches, arbitrary
Orders, lunch, fluorescent lights and styes?'
'Yes, darling, but not all the out-of-work
Have your resilience. Some kill themselves. Some others.
What about them?'
'I don't know.
Perhaps you're right. When I was younger
I believed that every human being
Had some gift, some gleaming, only buried
By dull teachers, honking politicians,
Television and the yellow press.
If they could find, could treasure up that spark . . .'
' . . . they'd perish like dogs on the road to the
poorhouse,'
Dear Andrea observed.
'Unemployment.'
I shuddered, thinking of more lines.
'The great blot on our name as reasonable,
Feeling, social creatures. But perhaps
The new technology, say, cryogenics—
We could freeze the unemployed until
Their services are needed, or until
Someone discovers what to do with them.'
Andrea giggled, 'Do you think there's a chance
We'll finally get snowbound this winter?'
A west wind stretched out all the flags
At the United Nations. Nearly home.
'Good evening, sir.' The doorman leaned
Against the door and handed me a package
From an undecided publisher.
And messages were on the phone machine.

'God, Sir.' Then She Was Quiet

Love answers
Fear. The drink
In the basin.
Come closer, the lens
Of the lowering sky.
Come closer. The breeze
Softly shakes
Down the dogwood, the wall
Of azaleas.
A grief and a pleasure.
The bee and the rose.

Prophylaxis

'It must have been exciting,
Having your father for a father:
He was always edgy, looking for adventure.
I remember once he came to see me
At the office. We discovered
Both of us had plans to spend that weekend
In the Catskills, and he said:
"Let's get together." That Saturday
We sat around the table having lunch—
Some other couple and your mother—
And your father said:
"I think I'll buy a car."
That afternoon he went down
Into town and bought a car:
That must have been three thousand dollars,
And he didn't even know the dealer.

'Why, my father used to take me
Around town with him, it could have been
Him walking a dog instead of me
For all that happened. I suppose it stuck.
Even when I was a teenager, horsing around
With my friends, and we would see
Who could make up some crazy stunt
For us to pull,
I couldn't think up even one. Not ever.
Know who I respect? Composers.
Writers start with something, have some model,
But composers pluck the sound out of thin air.

'There's an expression, it's called
"Stop the World, I Want to Get Off."

Well, that title really got to me.
I used to lead my life
Looking to other people to give me
Direction, never thinking that it might not be
Necessary to pursue the almighty dollar,
To do this or say that, and I became
—Don't think I mean too much by this—
A little odd, a bit out of the mainstream
And I have kept clear of business
Ever since. It puts a different slant
On things. You know,
There just might be a story in this,
The story of a man a little different,
Reflecting on the everyday, life's foibles.

'Have you had an X-ray lately?
Certain of my patients have developed
Cavities I've somehow overlooked
While probing with the instruments.
True, it's not good to over-radiate,
Yet it's possible to go too far
The other way. You have discomfort?
No? Then let's wait
Six more months. I know that money's
Short, and you'll be wanting it
For other things.
You may rinse now.'

This is God

This is God as an ageing Jewish man.
Note the moustache and the fringe of hair.
He has made some good investments
And is pretty well fixed,
But he has sorrows, too.
It's the sorrows made him
An ageing Jewish man.

The Land of Lookbehind

Bright snow plumes from the towers,
Covers the green church roof,
Powders the wrinkles on our ageing earth,
Dances solo in the birdless sky
And causes time to beat unearthly
Wings and spin the antic whispers
Stacked, and mild, and dry.

It was another age that danced
Between hazed trees to the fool's tune
Burbled, yellow sheaves, and grapes, and pipes
Because it was midsummer's eve,
And the sky wore flowing sleeves,
And the sun and moon and stars were duds
For the earth's green velvet pants.
So I turned from the world of deliberate fable,
Rose from the green knees of the earth,
And looked through glass beyond
The buildings to a white sky with parted
Pictures of years in the throes,
At those I loved who loved me
In rows, they bowed their grainy heads
And in their other thoughts turned away
As impatience does, when the curtains close.

Two Presents

The parrot Mephistopheles learned to call the cat
When he lived in the kitchen, and later mastered
'Cracker' and 'Hello.' The falcon in his yellow eye
Dilated at grapes, peeled carrots, but blanked at the
sunflower
Seeds he shelled in his foot. Five years of this
Until my father bought the bird a mate, Irvina,
His green double, even to the orange fringe
Above her beak. They fell in love, and after
A week-long courtship in the summer cage, they shared
One perch, a happy pair of half-moon parrots.
Although they made no egg, they called to the migrant
Birds that lit on the kitchen window. One December
Irvina died. Mephistopheles withdrew
To a corner of the cage and watched her carried off
In the business section of *The New York Times.*
A cloud of listlessness descended. He would not bite
A finger, but rather plucked at the pale
Green feathers on his breast continually, become
At last a naked, mournful devil. Removed
From view, the parrot lived another seven years
But never grew his feathers back, and would not talk,
And could not fly, as covered in a sheet
He whistled like an oriole, until.

The door swings on its hinges, a fly's wing
Without will or explanation. Walking down
57th Street, below the race of the adoring
Clouds, I don't feel connected to the crowds
And their concrete business, although I am.
Spacious, I remember Solomon Ibn Gabirol,
Born in Malaga, at an early age discovered

He had remarkable gifts. One generation
After his star set, it was written:
'None ever did his station reach;
He above his generation towered.'

The Giant Sun's Song

Who turned over in light
On the sky's soft floor,
The size of a leaf
That moved us so,
As Elizabeth's finger
Stirs the guitar strings.

Fateless, like the sleeping
Newborn, the sky breathes.
A cloud blooms, appoints
The buds and nodding
Always, touches what seems
The milk drunk stars.
They reel, always.

Yet it's given to us
Never to move from the spot.
Light dwindles, it falls
On pained men exchanging
The hours for hours
At a clip, as water
Dashed down the lip, long
Years into uncertainty.

Brown Cats in the Dog Days

I read a story yesterday:
The fox escapes the hounds
By the strength of his legs,
But the fox doesn't know this,
So he catches his breath
And preens his bushy tail.

'You have been more purely beautiful
Before than you are now,' she said.
And I thought: True. October lawns
The leaves held down, and flocks
Of migrants queued in vees, while clouds
Of sparrows eddy in the waveless oaks.
Full of days, the beakers broke in a blue shower
And now, you say, I sit and watch
The little sparks and toss them
Upward, my thoughts the fireflies
Of god, and grown.

In old Russia, an ironworker's father
Studied philosophy very hard, and found
A solution to the Great Question, which answer
He immediately carried to Tolstoy,
Who lived in a hut behind his great house
On the family lands. It was August.
The freed serfs had had enough
Of hoeing and weeding and reaping, and dozed
Below the sheaves, while the Count
Busied himself with his new world.
The philosopher leaned toward Tolstoy's ear.

'Yes,' said the Count, 'how pleasant it is,
But I do not expect to die.' And the sun
Dove into Europe, while wheat waved
To dogs in the wind. Then as now,
The world was almost over.
Brown cats curled by the teapots.
Peaches turned cantaloupe colors in the bowl.

In 1652 a rabbi dreamed
A camel pursued him from one room
To another. Though he locked the doors
With a complicated lock, the camel
Burst through and kept going.
At last the rabbi found himself
In a blue room by the ocean. There
He no longer feared the camel, and
A beautiful woman stepped out of the curtains
And kissed him. The sun set, the moon burned
As the sea came in through the window, and
'From fear and terror I awoke.'

But I slept by the sea
Without camels, while a man in a chair
Wrote a brief, and the words 'blue chip'
Flew off the page and skipped
South on the ocean, until all
I could see was the sea
And the mirroring sky.
Something is in it
Of the first days, then
Before the oceanic feeling was
The ocean, before streaks were drawn
Like giant airplanes travel, so fast
And high, less useful than disturbing.

Yesterday New York was clutched by a cloud
That swallowed all the scrannel noises
And turned the streets starling with blotches
Of brown, and the dusty accordion
Player who thinks of himself
As the Ancient of Days
Cursed a few quarter-tossers
In a language known only
To his accordion.
                    At times, the great beyond
Hangs fire, and everyone
Catches a breath, and it seems
Like something really will happen.
It does, of course, but not
So gaudy as thought. A quiet
Change, as an angel
Moving a wing through a century,
Waiting to be called.

Spring Fever

A moment in the clouds
Seen from the earth
When shafts of light bend down
To us, and the sun flares, the child
Called 'God in the clouds,' and growing
Thought, '200 years, such a short time, very long,'
And winding up slowly, started
To spin on the grass, and spun below
The clouds until falling, where
The earth was thought
To wheel about him, and the clouds
With time, too, and the blur
Of azaleas, an early feature of the spring.

3
The Exchange

Jingle

I've written poems on benches,
On the beach, in trains, in cars, on planes
Winging west and south, in bed
But most sitting at my desk, sober,
Drunk and walking up Broadway, drunk
And sitting on a stoop, sick, recovering,
In dire straits, in ecstasy, in stern moods,
Calm and panic, out of vanity, from hatred
Of my vanity, for vengeance, as rebuke,
Reply, riposte, return, thrust, stroke,
Caress and missile of an upset, poems
Of good and evil and the stuff that falls
Between them, falls like leaves
Or starlight from out there, sinking
To my knees or rising
To the drama of a small occasion, with wit
Or lackwit luster, clusters of love
Poems, wise poems, prose poems,
Poems of far ports and poems from homes,
    Rhymes and forms,
    Tunes in storms
    To cool madness,
    To expel sadness
    Like held breath,
    To do away with death
    (not possible) in life—
    Poems won me a sharp wife,
    A badly paid position,
    A view of the dust that clouds
    A view of the dust that clouds,
    A portable typewriter, ten cartons of books,
    The esteem of the powerless,

The love of the married,
The praise of professors,
Discounts from doctors,
A place with the gods
That no one believes in,
Some music on records,
A view of the sidewalk
From a wrought-iron balcony
Through French doors, high and airy
And a feeling the future
Will wake up and hug me
Like March air when the wind dies
And flowers fall open

So High, So Low

'I am remember the time, in Italy
Where Girolamo took my friend aside
(He couldn't say this to my face) he said
"Jimmy, he used to be a good radical
But America spoil him, he is not
Like me." What the hell. Forty,
Fifty years ago we all think, all
But me, "The Communist," but
Kropotkin, he say then, and I agree
That if the Communist keep going
(This was 1921) the way they go
In twenty year the world will come
To hate the name of Russia.

'But maybe I have changed, and maybe
None of us be what we think we are:
We want the money, we take it easy,
We get fat and grow the hair.
The children don't think how we do,
They don't want the dollar, but
They call themselves the radical. Pfui.
They call names at the police.
In Italy the priest and the policeman
Would kill you, and nobody waste his time
With names. One time when I work
On the ships (I just come to America)
I meet a friend, a anarchist, and he
Want me to run the whiskey with him
Because we fight together against
The Communist. "You must be crazy,"
I said. "You do this and you only find the trouble,
And what is your life then?"

'Henrietta, now
She's stopped the work, we both
Have time to go to opera. We watch
The television on the Watergate, but any country
That give you only two choice for the election
What can you expect? No difference
Between the one man and the other.
All of them make the people to hate
The name of government. Only the anarchist
Is any good. Only the anarchist, and I
Say this after more than seventy years living
And I always say this, like the Prince
Kropotkin say in 1921.'

Crusade Song

These feats of earth shall bring us to the air.
The past caught fright like colds
And old guitars hymn our libidos
Which guide us with Orlando and his birdbrain
Legions on to Bethlehem. The broad plain falls
Away from the Glum Mountains. Are we Turks
Or Huns or Tatars that we hang before the sack
With camels passing? Equals must remain
The same, even in the green and mortal eye
Our company berates the old administration
Who draw their bathrobes off beside the Jordan.

Leave us not grow torpid peccaries back home.
Our death is not so dear as what we know.
Nothing has been done anyway, for troubadours
To sing into a lady's hearth.
Remember history! Remember Scipio Africanus
And Alexander! Save your rice for bread
And can the marriage rites! There is a gauze
That overlies what shall be done, and your grandsons
Will look back to now with pleasure, thinking
Then, then men were men, there was revenge,
Adventure, and no foes besmirched the almanacs.

God leases out his salve. Our wounds will heal
With our hiccups, and the fright will pass
And we will rest, andirons, each with his fellow
And the fond boats will lie along the pillars
Rising and falling in the fans that turn the tides.
We shall be martyrs to the winds, the very winds that nightly
Crown the pines and meadows of our dear Provence.

At that fair house no churl dare to complain,
And the shepherd calls the Caliph's grandson, his retainer
To carry out the slops, or fan the forge
Which heats the blade that made the Moslem melancholy.

Our song sounds like the edges of the neap tide,
Our companions dressed like falcons poised to swoop,
Our marks the iron mountain and the lion,
We come like flames from Flanders to the flat grainfields here
And fire our French-forged lances at the spaces
Turk dogs dare to fill. Grr. A red and sober hour.
They'll wish they'd slept with cobras in their camp
Or straggled at the Bosporus and drowned
Rather than face the terrors of our conquest,
A face more terrible than twenty sieges without water in the Sudan
And the troops of Cæsar lurking at the gate.

Draw a pot for the collector of uproar.
Beware, o snake, beware the mailed heel.
Death, do not think to eat our company—
It's not your fate: we're all going
To Paradise, in style, like Elijah.
The passive mares of passage clear our way.

French horses, raised within the moated fastness
Nose their enemies aside with evening oats
And grazing as they go, 'til not one blade remains
Below the heavy bells around their necks
And death shall no more visit them, than shall the phoenix
Fly into the sun again, with all our company.

—after Raimbaut de Vaqueiras

The Wanderer

Someone wants mercy   for himself alone
The wind's favor   though he's sad
And through sea lanes   long and chilly
Stirs with his hand   the top of the cold sea
The wake of his exile: a man set in motion
The traveller talked   about ships, remembering
The wind's wrath, the war   where his friends fell:
I often sit alone   on the shore at sunrise
And care for what happened: no one alive
Knows what I know   none dare
The sea's clear days: but I know
Great men carry   something large
Inside them, a cloud   tied to the light
And his heart pounds   so he thinks what he can
And stands in that light   the sea wind breaks
Over yes and no   over help and anger
So great men, brilliant   know the heart's dull sound
Is the heart   the line
My mind reels in   from the minded sea
Often troubled   casting off from home
From friends and family   tied to the land
And her children, covered   so I left
Heavily, dragging tackle   a spar on frozen seas
Sought halls and treasure   and givers
Wherever I found   in far or near distance
A friend   some comfort
A party   whoever lives
Knows how poor   a friend sadness is
To someone who   has few friends
The thin exile   not a golden road.
The beaker is chilled   not as earth's glory
He remembers sharing   gold with his friends.

They were younger   were golden
Were singers and eaters   all past, gold, gone
So he who must, knows   his friends
The clear lessons   must go on without
What sorrow and sleep   tie together
That one bound   together alone:
He seems to remember   his father in fortune
May hug him and kiss him,   touch
Hands, knees and head   as once
Years past   he sat in power
That wakes him   man, friendless
To visions before him: the black waves
The gulls bathing   spreading white feathers
Frost under snow falling   mixed with hail
Then the hard parts   the heart holds
Laid open, the pair   born like tears
In the memory   the mind watches
And welcomes   looks over
Its early companions   swimming away
The clouds   do not carry
Words friends are saying—   care recalls
Those who would banish   too often
What waves bind   to the mind.

So I cannot think   of the world
While my mind   doesn't darken
When I think   of man's whole life
How it drops   through the floor
Proud retainers   in this world
Where all days come   to holes and falls.
Therefore a man may grow   wise before leaving
The portions of winter to   worlds waiting, wise
His heart will not heat   tongue will not hasten
War will not weaken   nor foolish
Nor fearful, nor   happy, nor hungry
Nor fast to boast   before he is certain

A man waits   to boast
Until armed and   striking, then he knows
How his heart's thoughts   turn out.
A wise man   sees withered
All this world's   wealth wasted
Flat on the plain   sand on the beach
Where wind sweeps   the walls stand
Frost-covered   snow fences
Fall around halls   falling on rulers
In ruins, the joy   of companions collapsed
By pride   some taken
By battle   some taken
By birds by   the high sea
The gray wolf   dealt death to
One, crying, in rock   cave, the man, hid.
Earth wasted   man's mother
Of music and dances   men, robbed of
The old works of giants   stopped, idled:
He then, using wisdom   considers the floor
And the deep   and dark life
In wise clouds   he remembers
Sowing and slaughter   and speaks:

Where did the horses go?   Where are the families?
Where the bright dinners   the presents, the parties?
O the bright cup   the fighter
O power of princes   time passes
Below the dark sail   of night, as if
Never a thread   a shard of the company
A very high wall   painted with serpents
The spears all   ran to us
The arrows were thirsty   for fate
As these stone cliffs   storms break
Snow falling   binds the earth
With white winter   cold tumult as dark
Darkens, the shadow   of night from the north

Drives the hail   in men's faces
All harsh   on the earth
And the course rolls   down under the world
Here property passes   here friends pass the sky
Here man passes   families passing
The floor of the earth   stops her threshing.

So spoke the wise man   he sat alone, thinking
A man is good   who holds to his truth
Nor should he mourn   too readily
Unless he knows   the remedy
To work with his heart   because rest comes
From the sky   to us all
As does mercy   as sure as we stand.

—from the Old English

Hastening Thus

When I was ten my family went to Europe,
Not with an organized tour group,

But in a Fiat. In Paris, however, we
Took a bus tour, which I remember distinctly:

Our first stop was the Montmartre
And Le Sacre Coeur (one place combining God and art

As was explained in four languages): the white
Cathedral rode a cloud above the mount, in the light

Of that August afternoon. Knowing nothing of absinthe,
I wasn't interested then in tales of bohemian poets and
  painters who lived a marginal but rich existence in
  those narrow streets at the turn of the last century,
  although I might be since.

We stopped next at Notre Dame in the Ile de France
(Until then I thought the Ile was just a boat.) By chance

A Latin service was in progress,
So after taking in the lost art of stained glass,

I left the church interior
And went back to the square,

Which brings me
To the focus of my memory.

Carved figures of the Saints occupy a cleft
In the church facade. Halfway up, to the left

Stands a carving of St Denis, his head under his arm—
This caused my younger sister some alarm.

An analogy with decapitated chickens was rejected
By us both, as well as several less compelling
explanations. Unperfected

Visions of the crucifixion haunted my sleep in Italy,
Along with other Catholic imagery,

But, among the urban scenery,
St Denis' head remains most prominent in my memory.

There also was a Europe without parents:
Riding horseback in Villeneuve, swimming at Clarens,

Riding the funicular between Montreux and Glion
To camp, which overlooked the Chateau de Chillon.

In the castle dungeon I saw the pillar
Where Byron carved his name (I thought he was the
prisoner),

And hikes above Glion, the rushing river and the rock
(Rochers des Nayes) where, on a small village green, a
clock

Face planted with summer blooms.
There is a corner in the rooms

Of memory, even when the sun stays, dark
And dreadful. There, where two walls intersect the floor,
a spark

Curves on the joint of three dimensions. Fear
And chaos, monsters from the id, all the crude mater-

Ials of life live there, and it was also in late August, on a
hike
In the Dents du Midi near the French border, that I saw
night

Crash into those red cliffs, and saw (quite literally) the
way
Space yawns. That day

We campers went out for a walk on a path
Threading the edge of a 3,000-foot cliff. Half

Of us marched single file toward the bluff that overlooked
the Tal.
The other half had turned back to make dinner. While

The sun dropped behind me I wished that I had brought
My camera, thinking 'These mountains are as they are
now once, and sought

For later never will appear as now.' But
I had left my camera at the lodge. Thinking like that,

One camper broke into a run, he ran
Downhill along the edge before us calling "Look, look"
and then

I knew that he would slip.
He hit a wet strip

On the path and toppled forward.
The mountains swim before a word

Can capture them, and that one shriek
I made then also rises from the corner, high and weak.

Later, back at the lodge, a counsellor lost
His watch, which he decided had been stolen. Most

Of the night we sat on wooden benches in the summer
chill
Waiting for the thief to confess. No one did. Until

The watch was found next to the Turkish toilet, we stayed
Awake. Since that day I have never played

Too close to the edge
Of any ledge,

Either a New York City
Roof, or rural gorge. I can be, and have been, witty

About annihilation, although it scares me.
And memory, while it halts, never impairs me

While hastening thus,
Minus or plus.

No Harm Done

The last day of July: the sun is out
And time seems many papers folded over—
Out, in the way a light goes out,
Relentless. But that imputes some sense to light

And time seems many papers folded over.
Perhaps some useful fact will come to light, something
Relentless. But that imputes some sense to light
Which has no sense, and has nothing to indicate.

Perhaps some useful fact will come to light, something
Navigable by the backward sense
Which has no sense, and has nothing to indicate
But, as a great sphere, meets my feet,

Navigable by the backward sense,
Across the smoky lawns and sidewalks of twenty years
ago.
But, as a great sphere meets my feet,
The trek is effortless and irresistible.

Across the smoky lawns and sidewalks of twenty years
ago,
The last day of July. The sun is out,
(The trek is effortless and irresistible)
Out in the way a light goes out.

A Very High Ceiling

I remember the night we met
Six years ago. Tall George
Told me Mr. Friendly's secretary
Was throwing a party, and as I knew her bassist
Friend, I decided to go.
Mild mid-November. I walked up
West End Avenue from my garden
Basement on West 83rd Street.

You stood in the kitchen with your mother,
I thought 'a doll' (small),
As I glimpsed you through the press.
You shook my hand and asked my name.
In love on the receiving line, I stayed
That way by taxi downtown with the recent
Divorcee, home and to sleep,
Then uptown next night after you returned
From working at the airline.
I said little as we sat for hours
In the West End bar. I woke up
Smiling to the morning clang of pipes
And trucks. The sun barked through its yellow bottle.
Planes flew up Broadway.

The days' parade. Your father, the munitions
Manufacturer; your mother drinking
Indiana in the Malamute Saloon;
The brothers, sisters, drunks or druggies;
You, the flower bent suns turned to;
Me, I was no help.
By late spring you stopped humming

Mountain music while you picked up
The apartment, left the airline, started
Working in the bar, and after work
Would stand off-center in a room and cry,
You said, for 'Everything is growing old.'
Back after a week of lakeside camping,
You told me how you dressed your mouse folk
In your childhood bedroom, calling for
'The moon, mother, mother, the moon.'

You never answered my long letters, neither
From the Church school in Jamaica where I taught
For half-a-year, nor from the Finger Lakes
Where I went north to study. Between those poles
You led me once back to our old apartment,
Held me at the door, said I seemed stronger,
More alive. I never crossed the threshold.
Once more, a later autumn at the bar
Before my wedding, you tugged my lapel
And said, 'How fine you look, how fine together,'
And turning to your glass, closed with
'I told you you were good.'

The sky is closer in the Colorado
Rockies, but no softer: winds pierce the pines
And walk the walls, the moon's eclipse
Brought mountain wolves into the open.
Married, sick, still thinking of you
I paid a pilgrim's visit to your bar
After Thanksgiving. Nick the bouncer
Saw me with his one good eye, and said
'There is only the infinity of nothingness to push for.'
I thought, 'Brother.' Then, 'You know she's dead?'
My first thought was no thought. Next came
'The pity.' Next, 'For years now she's been

Dead to me,' and then a gap,
And now this weekend morning.

I went out for a walk this afternoon
(Today turned out one of the warmer days)
And stopped on the bridge above Ithaca Falls
To stare at the flow. Tires made pocketing sounds
On the grid. Below, pigeons swooped
From ledge to ledge. I crossed the bridge and looked
Upstream, the way the shadows lengthened in
The gorge. On a rock at the edge
A girl moved in a long pink dress, twirling
And retreating from the spring flood.
She danced for minutes, when the shadows
Caught her, then she started for the steps
That brought her from the bottom to the lip.

Heimkunft

Still, a bright night in the Alps and the clouds
        Composed of fire cover the mouth of the yawning
                valley.
Here, there, the mountain winds roar and plunge
        Harsh and bounce, wind down through the pine
                where they dwindle to a single breath.
Deliberate, the twitching laugh rushes and thrashes—it is
                Chaos
        With his youthful profile. Still strong, he celebrates
                his favourite contest
Under the rocks, then ferments and reels into the eternal
                closet.
        Even drunkards drag themselves through morning.
Then, the evergreens, the year, the holy
        Hour and the day, align in greater order, fused.
The eagle, watching as it hangs
        In space between two mountains, cries.
Now the village wakes, and peers into the depths,
        Fearless, trusting height below the peaks.
Whispers of growth, like bolts, the old springs
        Fall, the ground misted in descent,
Echoes call echoes, and the immeasurable workshop
        Rules the arm day and night, presents dispatched.

Meanwhile, the silver heights prevail,
        Full of roses covered with luminous snow.
And still higher, above the lights, lives the immaculate
        Shade, whose pleasures are his holy rays.
He lives alone in quiet, and his face shines
        With the air, bent on giving life,
To make us happy, many times: when, versed in measures,

Versed also in the breath, halting and holding
Fortunes of cities and houses, the mild
Rain, to soften the earth, hatches from clouds, for us:
We trust the sky, who sends us spring.
With a slow hand sorrows smile again,
Since he renews the time: the author, the still
Hearts of long-gone singers fresh and beating,
Works in the deeps, which open and lighten
As he wishes, and life begins again. Now
Grace flowers, as before, and the presence, spirit comes—
A beaming mood expands his spreading arms.

I spoke of many matters with him, of the poetic sense
Or songs: this matters mostly to the angels and to him.
I asked, for the sake of my homeland, since
No selfish pleas are pleasant to the sky;
Also, I asked for those unhappy in our country:
To them, blessings come as uprooted smiles—
Countrymen! for us. Meanwhile, the tide rocks me
And the helmsman smokes quietly, praising the passage.
Far in the sea's narrows fortune's traveller points
Below the sails' billow toward the city
Glinting in the early sunlight, while the Alps tug
Their long shadows: a ship slips into port.
The riverbank is warm here, and familiar valleys
Stitched with footpaths, green and grown with meaning.
Neighbor gardens mass their sparkling buds,
And birdsongs invite the passing traveller in.
All's confidence, the short greeting
Also friendly—a large family of faces.

Released! here I was born, the floor of my homeland

And what you look for—it's close—it comes to meet you.
And I didn't just stand there like the sun on the gate
Girt by waves and gawk and reach for loving names for you
In songs, a traveller: Blessed Lindau!
This is one of the natural gates to the land
Luring me into the much-discussed distance.
There, where the wonders are, there, where the stag
Breaks tracks among the narrow ledges shouldering the Rhine
And the valley drags itself out of the rocks
And drops, through ice mountains that melt into Como,
Or sweeps, as the day moves, into the open sea;
But you are more attractive, gate with posts.
To go home, to the familiar walks,
To see the meadowlands, the valley of the Neckar,
And the woods, the green and sacred columns, where
The oak sways over birch and beech
And the mountains reach me in a fit of tenderness.

There it touches me. O voice of the city, my mother!
You meet me, you rule me with long knowledge.
Nonetheless, it's still you, the spark of sun and happiness.
O best beloved! and the eyes burn clear, as before.
Yes! it's the Age! It thrives and ripens as nothing else
That lives or loves, and permits trust to return.
But the greatest find which lies beneath the arch
Of peace, is that you keep both youth and age.
I'm talking nonsense. This is joy. Since tomorrow and the future
When we go and look out of the living field
Under the blooming trees, in spring's festival
I speak and hope with everyone for your love.

I've heard a lot about this great father, and have
Been silent with him too long, who refreshes wandering time
In the sky, and lords it over mountains.
He continues with his giving, calls
Clear songs and sends out gentle musings. O, don't wait:
Come, our preservation! Angel of the year! and you

Angel of the house, enter all the veins of life—
Everyone happy at once, a part of the sky.
Exalted! reborn! without you nothing human, not
An hour of the day without its blessing and also
Such joys as now, when loving finds itself.
As this belongs to you, it should be a holy gift.
When we bless the meal, what should I name? And when we
Rest from weekly life, how do I bring thanks?
Should I summon the sky? A god loves nothing unfit:
Our joy is too small to tempt him.
We must be silent. The holy names are absent.
Hearts beat. Do the words fly up or remain?
But a harp lends its tones to the hour,
And perhaps the sky is happy when the notes arrive.
This prepares, and so approaches, sorrow
Released, which travels underneath the song.
Sorrows such as these must, like it or not, seize
The singer often, and his song; but the others—no.

—Friedrich Hölderlin

Hymn to Creation

Jeremy Bentham, Fichte and God
Descended from a pseudopod.

Aquinas, Augustine, Pico della Mirandola
Didn't compose until out of the stroller

Unlike J S Mill and W A Mozart
Who practised as infants their chosen art.

William Shakespeare and John Milton
Grew up in England and slept with a quilt on.

Voltaire, Spinoza, Hegel, Rousseau,
Plato, Blake, Byron and Diderot,

Coleridge, Wordsworth, Dante Alighieri,
Rabelais, Jesus, Joseph and Mary:

All of these people and Moses and God
Descended from a pseudopod.

Affect

'It is refulgent,' said Rabbi Simeon, 'this child,
But he will not grow to be a great man.'
'Why?' asked his colleague, lighting a candle.
'Because so much light burns quickly, and at fifteen
He would be too old for a man. The stutterer,
The man with a few answers, endures to old age, and is
The great man among us.' The smoke rose
From the candle with his words; vented by the house they rose
Above the radio towers, above the twenty-storey office buildings, they rose
Conveniently beside an eagle, who kept them from falling.

Clouds

The little tennis ball and the handball blown with wind

Kestrels flagging on the western wind
The heaviness of time could be lightweight

Clouds pinned beneath a paperweight
The sky still perpendicular as I designed it
What beauty

There is no fault at the beginning of a world
Those measurements that don't quite reach the clouds,
curled
Up or dying suddenly at Pisa on the morning
Of a shoelace, or only swallowed clouds

The Roof

Here where the jetstreams rise,
The spine of the Continental Divide,
Halfway up a cliff, in air

His hammer keeping time,
His pitons marking climb,
A mountain climber sang this prayer:

I clamber on the edge of rocks
The negative of city blocks.
This granite no god's passive face

This ledge no human dwelling place
But here the small green lichen grow
In hollows worn by melting snow

And wind, it hustles through a day
And blows the fall away.

The bighorn sheep and mountain goats
Grow old upon these winter slopes.
Eagles hover in these peaks

No longer signs, as hours and weeks.
Clouds. The moon emerges from eclipse
To light the crusted, mossy lips

Of tundra spread below the glacier—
Snow without erasure.

The rose-hip of late summer,
Harebell, cowslip, columbine,
Strawberry blite, air rarified:

And if the wind rose, I'd lift
And smash my back against the cliff
Or if a cold front catches me

Ascending, I would freeze quickly.
What to possess?

Glacier, crevasse
The drop hard brass—
Listen, the hammer sinks the piton

And it rings.
                    My feet on
The short pegs I drive

Keep me alive.
All is mine.

Above the timber line.

This was the prayer the climber sung
While going up the granite cliff.
                    His line and hammer gave it lift
And held his body where it hung.

Three Generations at One Table on the Patio

Their faces weather in the picnic air.
A man lay down upon the ground.
'Between,' he said, 'the earth and air.'
The night diverges on a stair.
The wheel swings around.

Across the bottom of a hill
Old easy Jane and Horny Bill
Fill up an afternoon of chat.
A bentwood cane, a snapbrim hat.
A onetime full and empty chair.

Gertrude and Samuel

Not yet and still was English spoken.
        Der Schmied she sang, an organ
In her chest as well and 'O Sam,
        We could be happy.'
If textiles hold firm.
        Thence to purchase Tudor oaks
And a sweep of lawn beyond the city.

'Those drapes from Mrs. Whitney's living room.'
        The carved elephants from India, in ivory,
The lacquered chest, the Persian rugs,
        A genuine Louis XIV tapestry,
Silk ties, a spinet piano—
        'But all the recordings
Lost in a fire. The whole studio
        Went, you know.

'And I sang for the mayor
        On the radio,
In New York, Paris and Milan
        But the war ended all that
And then Sam wanted me
        To spend my time with the children.
We nine sisters were the toast of old New York.
        All so accomplished. Nellie and Bella and Henrietta
Although they had their children,
        They were jealous, I think, of my success.
But I have tried to be patient
        And do right by them.'

'I was the youngest of five children.
        I came here from Hungary when I was twelve
And immediately went to work.
        A Talmudic scholar, my father left the faith.
His wife, my mother
        Soaked our beef in brine.
My ambition, which I almost realized
        Twice, was to make a million dollars.
In '32, I sold out to Dunn and Bradstreet
        And went into imported fabrics.'

At a Bon Voyage party on the *Cristoforo Colombo*
        In 1953, my grandfather showed me a hundred-
                                                            dollar bill.
I said 'That's very big'
        Thinking 'A lot of money
In one place.' He said
        'This is not the first.'
Twelve years later and 'Gertrude,
        Bring me the nuts.
That book,' he said cracking a walnut
        With a walnut, 'is salacious.
Gray's *Elegy*, now that's
        What I call a poem.'

'We always liked the good things.
        Sam had his ties custom-made
In England—he always wore a vest:
        We always knew the best people.
We are comfortable now, having led
        A full life, and although it gets
Hard for me to care for Sam (he's always
        So demanding) yet we have
Our children and our grandchildren.'

The Good Life

Get up at ten o'clock, eat a little breakfast,
        Go down to the sea with a towel.
Take a little sun in a fifty-dollar chair,
        Then take a quick dip in the ocean.
                Drink a glass of planter's punch,
                Take a little sail, lunch,
                        Ski a little water ski.
Drive home after dinner with three tourist ladies
        And show them the sights with the top down.
Stop off at a bar,
        Drink a nightcap, then
                Go home and sleep
                        Until breakfast.

Water is the Mother of Ice

1

Then love introduces the expensive dream
Of peace into this last report on the future

Of the past, as the pen snaps
Into the gentle discipline.

If it weren't necessary to eat, I wouldn't
And if I didn't have to brace

Myself against fire and ice I would
By all means, relax.

But it's that negligence which leaves the body
Open and the hand gasping for comfort

In the middle of nightmares: certainly
I have lived too long in an atmosphere of hatred.

Discipline propels me through the social superstructure
Insisting 'stop and think, pick and choose'

While nothing is satisfied,
Not morning's bleary mirror

Or the later mirror of this afternoon.
This afternoon is colored natural to life.

This afternoon is warranted to neither fade nor spot.
This afternoon is excelled by none in the Union.

It presents the likenesses of children
In from two to four seconds, sitting

And I will not flatter my humble self—
It is a lot better than I am.

Improvements in poetry have not matched
Corresponding improvements in business,

And my life presents an even further halting:

2

What I want compares to the ancients
Who kept records on slabs of stone,

Aiming for a permanence which I
Can only dream of.

Faces flip past like pictures in a book,
Too fast to take a closer look, but

Not fast enough to be ignored.
It doesn't pay to go out for a walk.

It leaves me describing my condition
In leaves or flocks of birds, my feelings

Taking on the aspect of a mountain or river,
Massive, natural, subject to the sun and moon,

Independent of the will. The will
Implies both a future, and a backward glance:

The wishes of the dead are remarkably strong:
They are the breezes of the present life

And buffet the living, like leaves or flocks
Of birds migrating north after a long winter

To cooler regions. And these breezes which intend
To abolish chance create it, and although

The winds can be felt, they too are invisible
As chance, electric, the probable air.

What do I want? I want to leave
Something behind me which is not will,

Which does not challenge the workings of the planets
Or the heart, but includes them, and chance as well

In a breath. Water is the mother of ice
And land of the fish. The sun

Is the mask of evening. Ice, bark of the rivers
And vault of the waves visits in a cold time

And vanishes in a hot season, which equals
The sun. I keep the dull and weekly hours,

Record the natural equations, and decorate
The earth with songs to draw the strings

Of my relations, which tie me to other men,
To the earth, my own body, and the stars.

It is four o'clock in the afternoon.

The Exchange

At first, the sky included the earth.
When the sun and stars came out, the sky
Took the earth and put her in her place.
The earth, separated from the sky, was dumbfounded
And amazed: she wanted to get out of the dark.
At last, the sun climbed up and looked in her face.
And so the earth was firmly established.
And that is where we stand today.

I looked up at the sky and said
Sky, do you have any good ideas?
But the sky answered 'Not tonight.'
If you talk to the sky it will
Always answer in this way.
Sometimes it answers 'Not today.'

Hymn

The world of the wind was woven warp and woof on the
strands of a guitar whose heart lives in the lost cities
of foreign scripture fame whose words come from
the fire of the female species whose heart warms
the words within the cities where harps revise the
passage of wind which is the breath of

the cows grazing in the far corner of the common in the
northern entrance to the city whose map is carried
by the people of the city behind their ribs which
feeds the fork where the fire lives which bears the
city across the wind weaving warp and woof.

This creation speculation sometimes was a pre-cosmic
person whose daughter's baby was his son which
broken into fragments became the universe. A goat,
he couples with a goat. She is a horse, he becomes a
stallion and the world a colt. And so it goes. The
creatures of the air hymns were born from this
emitted female. And nothing was missing. And there
was no original.

The End of Autumn

From time to time all
the gardens are not the same:
from the gilded to the golden
a slow dissociation:
that's how it's been on my street:
watching the old men creeping up on breath,
the teenagers swimming in the silver wash.

Ode

1

It's quiet in the suburbs; the lighted streets don't move.
The cars drive past, decorated with facts.
Satisfied men walk home from work, to silence.
The sensible roofs bear the weight of prizes and ambition,
And the houses are well satisfied. Emptied of grapes and flowers
And clerks and shoppers, the supermarket rests.
But a guitar may be heard in the backyard. Perhaps
Some lover is playing, or some single man
Who thinks about distant friends and his 'teens. And sprinklers
Ascend and rush fresh across smoky lawns.
A clock sounds through the still dimming air,
And the thought of hours calms a watcher of numbers.
Now comes movement, and the supremacy of rooftops.
Look, the earth's shadow, the moon
Makes a secret appearance. Insect swarms, the night comes
Full of stars and a bit sorry for us.
Those who are surprised look up. They are the small foreigners among men.
They see over mountaintops.

2

Tall men possess a wonderful grace, and no one
Knows about their wants, and their effects.
So they move the world, and are moved—optimists

Don't understand the signs themselves. They
prepare, because
The sky wants them to. The sky loves you. Because of this
It prefers you to daylight, as you do yourself.
At the same time, a clear eye also loves shadows,
And tries to find sleep before it becomes an effort.
Or, it looks out in the night for a real man.
Yes, it is appropriate to pursue flowers and poetry,
Because the sky favors the misguided. And the dead
Themselves invariably exist in free vapors.
But you must also be for us, in the spaces,
Accessible in the dark.
Decant lost memory and euphoria,
Decant streams of words, which exist in
Sleepless lovers, full pitchers, the lives of insects—
These too are important thoughts.

3

The heart is lost in ribs. Only
We keep our temper, father and son. Who
Would stop us? Who wants us to be unhappy?
Fire tries to decompose, both in daylight and
evening hours.
Come on. We see the opening,
The one we are looking for. It's miles away.
One remains secure. It's the same in daylight
And at night. One is the measure
Common to everything. Try it, it divides itself.
Each division leads where it can—
There, for instance. Laughter enjoys long-haired insanity,
When it seizes the singer after dark.
On to the Isthmus, where the open water journeys
To Parnassus, and snow deflects oracular stones.

There, in the land of Olympus, there on Cithæron,
Under the figs, the grapes, dates, olives, where
Thebes declines and Ismenos hurries into the land of
Cadmos,
This is the source, the returning index of an
impending order.

4

Greece, house of the sky,
Is it true, what we heard in early childhood?
A small vestibule; the sea—the floor; the mountains—the
table:
A singular monument to antique architecture.
Where are the chaises, the temple, and the pitcher
Of orange juice, the artifacts of inspired poetry?
Where is the light of wandering speech?
Sleeping, isn't Delphi disturbed by universal history?
Where is speed? Where does contemporary luck fail?
Thunder is distilled in chaste air, and dominates the
eyes.
Euphoria is the common property of tongues,
As it cannot survive alone.
The products are divided and distributed among
foreigners
At the party. The power of words breathes, grows
sleepy:
The tongue manufactures echoes, which, deflected,
approach
Old signs left by our grandfathers.
In this way the sky returns, a great success
In the shadows which support men in daylight.

5

Insensitivity comes first. It fights with
The kids, struggles with streetlights, mixes with luck,
But keeps shy of real men. They preserve
The names, which they guard like Christmas presents.
They keep their temper, and it fills their hearts
With great occasions. They know how to hold on to products—
Manufactured, found, lost and abandoned.
Their hands are educated to move earth and alloys.
It's possible the sky has a hand in this. But to tell the truth,
They come and settle on their own. They are the sons of luck
And days, and they see every opening. Their faces
Name everything and anything, one and many.
Their ribs conceal abundance,
And they are first and alone when anything succeeds.
They are real men. When products and presents
Replace the sky, then nothing is seen or known.
This is a burden. Now the sky names its lover.
For this reason, words must resist like flowers.

6

Now he thinks seriously about honor:
Praise is not to be taken lightly.
Nothing which offends the sky may see light:
Is euphoria therefore an obligation?

In order to deserve the sky's presence,
        People compare themselves to existing standards,
And order themselves in layers. They build temples and
                                        suburban houses,
        Parks and swimming pools, sidewalks and
                                        streetlights.
Where are they? Where does friendship bloom? In lighted
                                        playgrounds?
        Thebes wilts; so does Athens. The weapons have left
Olympus. We are left with the movement of gold bicycles.
        There are no flowers on the ships of Corinth.
Why were you quiet, outside, after the movie?
        Why were you happy when the dancing started?
Why are the street signs like faces instead of signs?
        Why is the kitchen stocked with free samples?
Or, he comes to his senses, gathers his shadow,
        Puts out the empties, and leaves for the party.

7

Well, my friend, you're too late. Everybody's alive.
        They're up on the roof, in another world.
They meet with endless success, appearing to look up
        At the stars, as if alive, as if the sky were a mirror.
This cannot be done with weak eyes,
        As time, at times, is full up with men.
Dreams supply the rest. But error helps,
        As does sleep, which strengthens both the need and
                                        the night.
Until the heroes leave their strollers and grow up,
        Expanding their hearts, they only resemble daylight.
Thunder usually accompanies them. At such times, I
                                        prefer
        To sleep, to be without pleasure or illusion.
I don't know what to do about this, or what to say.

Neither do poets, even in permissive times.
But you say that they are the agents of Bacchus,
Travelling from town to town on night trains, in buses.

8

Eventually, at certain times, they cover us with darkness.
Everyone ascends, bathed in fortune,
Just as fathers relate to men's faces.
With this, the earth begins in sadness and right,
Until the appearance of a quiet genius. He meets with
The sky, acquaints himself with the solstice, the zenith, the equator and the horizon,
Leaving marks on lamp-posts, letting us know
He's been here, and will be here again. He returns all gifts
And introduces us to daylight.
Through happiness, through thought, the universe expands and contracts
Beneath our feet. Unfortunately, æsthetes miss the higher
Joys, which live quietly, in gratitude.
Bread is the earth's fruit: it rises in the light.
And the pleasures of wine come from the thunder.
For this reason, we consider the sky, which visits once
And comes again at the proper time.
For this reason we take our songs seriously; the singer, Bacchus:
There is a good reason for grandfathers to expect our praise.

These Anemones, Their Song Is Made Up as They Float Along

In 1954, in June
I saw a total eclipse of the sun by the moon.
I saw the flowers fold up, the birds
Stopped singing to the morning, the grass
Grew wet, and it was dark.
I was awake, but when I was awake
A while longer I woke up and said
'I have slept until now,' and now
I have stopped sleeping altogether.